"Marked by T. Desmond Alexander's typica[...] exegesis, *The City of God and the Goal of Cre[...] theology that sets forth how the narrative of [...] Jerusalem, where God's people will enjoy a li[...] book for yourself and get it for others too."

Michael Morales, Professor of Biblical Studies, Greenville Presbyterian Theological Seminary; author, *The Tabernacle Pre-Figured* and *Who Shall Ascend the Mountain of the Lord?*; editor, *Cult and Cosmos: Tilting toward a Temple-Centered Theology*

"At a time when worldwide urbanization—the movement of people from country to city—is at full flood, many think of cities not only as centers of jobs, culture, and government, but as sinkholes of iniquity. This interesting book competently introduces us to the theme of *city* in the Bible, tracing out its trajectory through Scripture and its promise for the future, and takes us finally to the New Jerusalem from which sin and all its effects are forever banished."

D. A. Carson, Research Professor of New Testament, Trinity Evangelical Divinity School; Cofounder, The Gospel Coalition

"This fascinating short study provides a splendid overview of the Bible's teaching on the city of God, tracing its early beginnings in the garden of Eden and following it all the way to its culmination in the New Jerusalem. This is biblical theology at its best. A magnificent study!"

Andreas J. Köstenberger, Senior Research Professor of New Testament and Biblical Theology, Southeastern Baptist Theological Seminary; Founder, Biblical Foundations

"Readers are helped to grasp not only the significance of a key biblical topic but also how Scripture contains a coherent storyline and consistent message. Filled with numerous theological insights, this is a must-read for anyone looking for an informed and reliable discussion."

Paul Williamson, Lecturer in Old Testament, Moore Theological College, Sydney, Australia; author, *Sealed with an Oath* and *Death and the Afterlife*

"New believers trying to make sense of Scripture for the first time, as well as believers who have studied the Bible for decades, will find insight and encouragement in these pages. *The City of God and the Goal of Creation* is a feast for those who love the Word of God."

Keith A. Mathison, Professor of Systematic Theology, Reformation Bible College

"Alexander has achieved something marvelous here: many who study the big picture are skimpy on the details, while many who focus on the details miss out on the big picture—but here we have someone knowledgeable, thoughtful, judicious, and persuasive on the details and the big storyline."

> **C. John Collins,** Professor of Old Testament, Covenant Theological Seminary; author, *Did Adam and Eve Really Exist?*; Old Testament editor, *ESV Study Bible*

"This book brings together an astonishing number of Bible passages into a clear and coherent overview of the great narrative of the Bible."

> **Douglas Moo,** Kenneth T. Wessner Chair of Biblical Studies, Wheaton College; Chair, Committee on Bible Translation for the NIV

"*The city of God* is a central biblical theme, and T. Desmond Alexander masterfully guides us as he follows the theme from Genesis to Revelation. His study is a marvelous demonstration of the organic coherence of the Bible's message. I enthusiastically recommend this book to all Christians."

> **Tremper Longman III,** Distinguished Scholar of Biblical Studies, Westmont College

"I love this book! It may be short, but it packs a big punch. It is a book to savor—small in size, but bursting with biblical insights."

> **Jason Meyer,** Pastor for Preaching and Vision, Bethlehem Baptist Church, Minneapolis, Minnesota

"Despite the depressing state of the world, T. Desmond Alexander's biblical theology of Jerusalem provides a biblical basis for hope for the future. This is an irenic, fair, and easily accessible study of Jerusalem, the city of God."

> **Michael Rydelnik,** Professor of Jewish Studies and Bible, Moody Bible Institute; Host and Bible Teacher, *Open Line with Dr. Michael Rydelnik*, Moody Radio

"We are seeking the city that is to come, and there is no one I would rather read on the topic than T. Desmond Alexander. Read this book, then buy a stack of copies to give away."

> **James M. Hamilton Jr.,** Professor of Biblical Theology, The Southern Baptist Theological Seminary; author, *God's Glory in Salvation through Judgment*

The City of God and the Goal of Creation

Short Studies in Biblical Theology

Edited by Dane C. Ortlund and Miles V. Van Pelt

The City of God and the Goal of Creation, T. Desmond Alexander (2018)

Covenant and God's Purpose for the World, Thomas R. Schreiner (2017)

Divine Blessing and the Fullness of Life in the Presence of God, William R. Osborne (2020)

From Chaos to Cosmos: Creation to New Creation, Sidney Greidanus (2018)

The Kingdom of God and the Glory of the Cross, Patrick Schreiner (2018)

The Lord's Supper as the Sign and Meal of the New Covenant, Guy Prentiss Waters (2019)

Marriage and the Mystery of the Gospel, Ray Ortlund (2016)

The New Creation and the Storyline of Scripture, Frank Thielman (2021)

Redemptive Reversals and the Ironic Overturning of Human Wisdom, G. K. Beale (2019)

The Royal Priesthood and the Glory of God, David S. Schrock (2022)

Sanctification as Set Apart and Growing in Christ, Marny Köstenberger (2023)

The Serpent and the Serpent Slayer, Andrew David Naselli (2020)

The Son of God and the New Creation, Graeme Goldsworthy (2015)

Work and Our Labor in the Lord, James M. Hamilton Jr. (2017)

The City of God and the Goal of Creation

T. Desmond Alexander

Dane C. Ortlund and Miles Van Pelt,
series editors

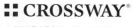

WHEATON, ILLINOIS

Trade paperback ISBN: 978-1-4335-5574-9
ePub ISBN: 978-1-4335-5577-0
PDF ISBN: 978-1-4335-5575-6
Mobipocket ISBN: 978-1-4335-5576-3

Library of Congress Cataloging-in-Publication Data

Names: Alexander, T. Desmond, author.
Title: The city of God and the goal of creation / T. Desmond Alexander.
Description: Wheaton : Crossway, 2018. | Series: Short studies in biblical theology | Includes bibliographical references and index.
Identifiers: LCCN 2017010292 (print) | LCCN 2017045265 (ebook) | ISBN 9781433555756 (pdf) | ISBN 9781433555763 (mobi) | ISBN 9781433555770 (epub) | ISBN 9781433555749 (tp)
Subjects: LCSH: Cities and towns—Biblical teaching. | Cities and towns in the Bible. | Cities and towns—Religious aspects—Christianity. | Eschatology.
Classification: LCC BS680.C5 (ebook) | LCC BS680.C5 A44 2018 (print) | DDC 220.6/4—dc23
LC record available at https://lccn.loc.gov/2017010292

Crossway is a publishing ministry of Good News Publishers.

BP			33	32	31	30	29	28	27	26	25	24	23
15	14	13	12	11	10	9	8	7	6	5	4	3	

For
Brian and Lesley McGlaughlin
Robert and Rosemary Wallace

Contents

Series Preface

Most of us tend to approach the Bible early on in our Christian lives as a vast, cavernous, and largely impenetrable book. We read the text piecemeal, finding golden nuggets of inspiration here and there, but remain unable to plug any given text meaningfully into the overarching storyline. Yet one of the great advances in evangelical biblical scholarship over the past few generations has been the recovery of biblical theology—that is, a renewed appreciation for the Bible as a theologically unified, historically rooted, progressively unfolding, and ultimately Christ-centered narrative of God's covenantal work in our world to redeem sinful humanity.

This renaissance of biblical theology is a blessing, yet little of it has been made available to the general Christian population. The purpose of Short Studies in Biblical Theology is to connect the resurgence of biblical theology at the academic level with everyday believers. Each volume is written by a capable scholar or churchman who is consciously writing in a way that requires no prerequisite theological training of the reader. Instead, any thoughtful Christian disciple can track with and benefit from these books.

Each volume in this series takes a whole-Bible theme and traces it through Scripture. In this way readers not only learn about a given theme but also are given a model for how to read the Bible as a coherent whole.

We are launching this series because we love the Bible, we love the church, and we long for the renewal of biblical theology in the academy to enliven the hearts and minds of Christ's disciples all around the world. As editors, we have found few discoveries more thrilling in life than that of seeing the whole Bible as a unified story of God's gracious acts of redemption, and indeed of seeing the whole Bible as ultimately about Jesus, as he himself testified (Luke 24:27; John 5:39).

The ultimate goal of Short Studies in Biblical Theology is to magnify the Savior and to build up his church—magnifying the Savior through showing how the whole Bible points to him and his gracious rescue of helpless sinners; and building up the church by strengthening believers in their grasp of these life-giving truths.

Dane C. Ortlund and Miles V. Van Pelt

Preface

This book is designed to provide a succinct overview of the biblical teaching on the concept of the city of God. The subject spans both Testaments and intersects with a significant number of other important topics, beginning with the garden of Eden in Genesis and coming to ultimate fulfillment in New Jerusalem. Some aspects of this topic are addressed more sparingly than others. If every possible avenue was explored fully, the present study would easily run into thousands of pages. Hopefully, a sense of balance has been achieved in selecting the content to be discussed. On occasion pointers are given in footnotes to topics and resources that could helpfully be explored further to flesh out what is said here.

I am grateful to Dane Ortlund and Miles Van Pelt for inviting me to contribute to this series, Short Studies in Biblical Theology, and for their helpful comments as editors. Their invitation has provided an excellent opportunity to write on this amazing subject. I am also indebted to Justin Young for constructive feedback on a first draft of the manuscript. For seeing this volume into print, special thanks go to the publishing team at Crossway. Throughout my academic life I have enjoyed the loving support of my wife, Anne. Her constant and faithful love has been for me and many others a wonderful testimony to the grace of God.

It is my prayer that this short book will inspire each reader to embrace wholeheartedly the psalmist's desire:

> One thing have I asked of the LORD,
>   that will I seek after:
> that I may dwell in the house of the LORD
>   all the days of my life,
> to gaze upon the beauty of the LORD
>   and to inquire in his temple. (Ps. 27:4)

Soli Deo Gloria

Introduction

Cities inspire very different emotions in people. For some they are a magnet, offering every opportunity and pleasure that a civilized person might desire. For others, cities are places from which to escape, the peace and tranquility of rural life being a more attractive alternative. Like them or loathe them, cities have been a pervasive feature of human life for millennia. Given their ubiquitous nature, it is no surprise that cities figure prominently in the Bible. Their presence, however, is not merely incidental. At the very heart of God's plan for our world stands an extraordinary city.

Exiled to the island of Patmos in the first century AD, the apostle John experienced a series of visions. He later recorded these in the book of Revelation as a message of encouragement to the earliest followers of Jesus Christ. John's final vision involves a city, but it is no ordinary metropolis. Its dimensions alone set it apart. Each side of its length, breadth, and height measures some 1,380 miles or 2,220 kilometers, far exceeding in size any known city, ancient or modern. Its enormity is matched by its grandeur. It is constructed of gold, with enormous walls of jasper decorated with twelve kinds of precious stones (Rev. 21:18–20). John's brief description conveys something of the city's opulence. Its magnificence almost places it beyond imagining.

Adding an altogether different aspect to this unique city, John observes that its citizens enjoy an environment transformed by the radiant presence of God himself. In this paradise city, peace, security, and wholeness are the nutrients of human flourishing. Evil is banished entirely, as humanity shares this idyllic conurbation with the divine Creator. This is a city like no other city.

This picture of an astonishing, other-world city is laden, like John's other visions in Revelation, with symbolic imagery drawn from the rest of Scripture. The abundance of these allusions adds to the sense that this vision reveals God's ultimate goal for humanity. This New Jerusalem is a fitting climax to the entire biblical story. As we shall explore in the chapters that follow, God has graciously and patiently been working to create this spectacular city, where he will dwell in harmony with humanity.

New Jerusalem and the Garden of Eden

New Jerusalem brings to completion what God intended when he first created the earth. Two acts of divine creation frame the Bible, and the links between them are far from superficial. The origins of New Jerusalem are to be found in the early chapters of Genesis. As we shall discover, the garden of Eden is located at the center of a green field site where God intends to construct a holy city upon the earth.

At first sight the garden of Eden does not appear to have much in common with New Jerusalem. Set side by side they seem to illustrate well a sharp contrast between rural and urban existence. Yet several features suggest that they are closely connected. First, and most unique, both locations are associated with the "tree of life." In Genesis the "tree of life" stands in the middle of the garden surrounded by many other plants (Gen. 2:16–17). While little is said about this tree, it clearly had the potential to give immortality. After Adam and Eve betray God and are expelled from Eden, God deliberately prevents them from accessing this life-giving tree (Gen. 3:22–24). Revelation 22 presents a very different situation, for the leaves of the "tree of life" are freely available for the healing of the nations (v. 2). This life-changing tree is mentioned nowhere else in Scripture, strongly suggesting that the two locations are closely linked.

Second, only in the biblical accounts concerning the garden of Eden and New Jerusalem do God and humans communicate directly with each other, face-to-face. Throughout the rest of Scripture attention is drawn to the alienation between God and people. The divine-human relationship was tragically broken when Adam and Eve were expelled from the garden of Eden. The situation described in New Jerusalem involves the restoration of this relationship. Only in the garden of Eden and New Jerusalem do God and humanity coexist in perfect harmony.

These links between the garden of Eden and New Jerusalem offer a basis for exploring further the idea that God's plans for humanity in Genesis 1–2 are orientated toward the creation of a unique city. Two lines of investigation offer additional support for this idea. First, there is among biblical scholars a growing recognition that the Eden narrative contains features that link it with later Israelite sanctuaries, especially the tabernacle and the Jerusalem temple. This is in keeping with the idea that God intends to dwell on the earth. Second, in Genesis 1 God instructs humans to be fruitful and multiply and fill the earth. This points toward the eventual creation of a worldwide community. While the early chapters of Genesis do not explain why people should fill the earth, the expectation is created that God and humanity will subsequently live together on earth in harmony. But, as we shall see, a tragic event catastrophically undermines progress toward this end.

Before expanding on these two related topics, an important observation needs to be made briefly regarding the interpretation of

Genesis 1–3. These chapters exhibit a concise narrative style and are limited in what they communicate. With minimum detail, the opening chapters of Genesis set the scene for all that follows. Consequently, these chapters contain examples of proleptic ambiguity; ideas are introduced briefly, with the expectation that these will be developed more fully in the subsequent narrative. The ongoing story clarifies what may initially be ambivalent or vague in Genesis 1–3. For this reason, it is important to read and understand the opening chapters of Genesis in light of what follows them. Unfortunately, too often scholars attempt to explain the subtleties of Genesis 1–3 without giving sufficient consideration to the remainder of Genesis.

Recent research on the opening chapters of Genesis has drawn attention to various ways in which the garden of Eden resembles later Israelite sanctuaries.[1] The entrances to Eden and later sanctuaries are located to the east and guarded by cherubim (Gen. 3:24; Ex. 25:18–22; 26:31; 36:35; 1 Kings 6:23–29; 2 Chron. 3:14). When God commands the man "to work it [the garden] and keep it" (Gen. 2:15), he uses the verbs *ʿābad*, "to serve, till," and *šāmar*, "to keep, observe, guard." Elsewhere in the Pentateuch these verbs are used in combination to describe the duties of the Levites in the sanctuary (cf. Num. 3:7–8; 8:26; 18:5–6).[2] Adam's role in the garden has Levitical connotations; he is to be a guardian of sacred space and not merely a gardener.

Other features of the Eden narrative may also be linked to later sanctuaries, although these connections are more tentative. On their own they do not carry much weight, but cumulatively they offer a consistent picture. The Jerusalem temple is decorated with arboreal features. The tabernacle menorah (or lampstand) resembles in shape

1. Gordon J. Wenham, "Sanctuary Symbolism in the Garden of Eden Story," *Proceedings of the World Congress of Jewish Studies* 9 (1986): 19–25.

2. Umberto Cassuto, *Commentary on Genesis*, 2 vols. (Jerusalem: Magnes Press, 1964), 1:122–23.

a tree, possibly representing the "tree of life" (Gen. 2:9; 3:22; cf. Ex. 25:31–35).[3] The mention of gold and onyx in Genesis 2:11–12 may be linked to the fact that gold, in particular, was used extensively to decorate Israelite sanctuaries and priestly garments (e.g., Ex. 25:7, 11, 17, 31). Although the gold and onyx lie outside the garden of Eden, mention of their location indicates that there is a known source for these materials. The LORD God walks in the garden of Eden as he later does in the tabernacle (Gen. 3:8; cf. Lev. 26:12; Deut. 23:14; 2 Sam. 7:6–7). The concept of a river flowing out of Eden (Gen. 2:10) finds a parallel in Ezekiel 47:1–12, where a river flows from a future, idealized Jerusalem temple, bringing life to the Dead Sea. The garden of Eden occupies an elevated location, a feature that recalls how other sanctuaries associate God's presence with an elevated location.

These parallels between the garden of Eden and later Israelite sanctuaries are hardly coincidental. Two possible interpretations may explain this. Either Eden is a protosanctuary, and other sanctuaries are modeled upon it,[4] or each later sanctuary is a restored garden of Eden.[5] If this latter option is adopted, the question arises, why replicate the garden of Eden? The most likely answer is that Eden recalls a time when humanity enjoyed an especially close relationship with God in an idyllic environment. Later sanctuaries replicate something of this experience as people come to the place where God dwells on earth. As a divine residence, the sanctuary enables God to live in close proximity to people. The text of Genesis does not state unambiguously that God dwells in Eden, but the impression is given

3. Carol L. Meyers, *The Tabernacle Menorah: A Synthetic Study of a Symbol from the Biblical Cult*, vol. 2, ASOR Dissertation Series (Missoula, MT: Scholars Press, 1976), 169–72.

4. E.g., G. K. Beale, *The Temple and the Church's Mission: A Biblical Theology of the Dwelling Place of God*, New Studies in Biblical Theology 17 (Downers Grove, IL: IVP Academic, 2004), 66–80.

5. Daniel I. Block, "Eden: A Temple? A Reassessment of the Biblical Evidence," in *From Creation to New Creation: Biblical Theology and Exegesis*, ed. D. M. Gurtner and B. L. Gladd (Peabody, MA: Hendrickson, 2013), 3–29.

that Eden is a place where potentially God and humanity will live together. In the beginning the garden of Eden has only two human resi-
dents and is clearly not a city. But as the human population increases
through time, Eden has the potential to become a great metropolis.[6]

The relationship between the garden of Eden and later sanctuaries
may be approached from another direction. The Israelite tabernacle,
and later the Jerusalem temple, was considered to be a microcosm or
model of the earth. In this capacity it provided a visual illustration,
anticipating God's glorious presence filling the whole world. This
expectation comes to fulfillment in New Jerusalem. As Revelation 21
reveals, New Jerusalem has no temple building, "for its temple is the
Lord God the Almighty and the Lamb" (Rev. 21:22). Viewed from the
perspective of God's presence filling the whole earth, the garden of
Eden represents the first stage toward the creation of New Jerusalem.

From Garden to City

The garden of Eden narrative anticipates God and humanity dwelling
together in harmony. In light of this, the earliest readers of Genesis
would easily have expected Eden to become a temple-city. Familiar-
ity with ancient Near Eastern temples would have supported this
idea, for ancient temples were constructed at the heart of cities, the
human population serving the needs of the god who was in their
midst.

The expectation that Eden should become a temple-city fits well
with God's instruction that humans should "be fruitful and multiply
and fill the earth" (Gen. 1:28). While the intention of this instruction is obvious, no explicit explanation is given as to why this should
happen. The theme itself recurs throughout Genesis, being repeated

---

6. Cf. William J. Dumbrell, "Genesis 2:1–17: A Foreshadowing of the New Creation," in
Biblical Theology: Retrospect and Prospect, ed. S. J. Hafemann (Downers Grove, IL: InterVarsity
Press, 2002), 53–65.

twice to Noah after the flood (Gen. 9:1, 7) and echoed in the divine promise of numerous descendants given to the patriarchs, Abraham, Isaac, and Jacob (Gen. 12:2; 15:5; 17:6; 22:17; 26:4; 32:12; 35:11; 48:4; cf. Gen. 28:3; 47:27). In Genesis 1–2 the impression is conveyed that the boundaries of the garden will expand outward as the human population increases. This emphasis upon filling the earth points toward a large population, appropriate for a city.

God's future plans for Adam and Eve are closely tied to their status as his vice-regents. The final part of Genesis 1 emphasizes God's instructions that humans should exercise authority over all other creatures: the birds of the sky; the fish of the sea; every creature that moves along the ground. The importance of this instruction is underlined by its repetition in Genesis 1:26–28.

Humanity's God-given authority to rule over other creatures takes on special significance in light of what happens in Genesis 3. At the heart of the Serpent's encounter with Adam and Eve is a challenge to their status as God's vice-regents. Instructed by God to rule over all other creatures, they succumb to the Serpent's innuendos and accept what it has to say as trustworthy. Consequently, Adam and Eve willfully betray God, disregarding his instructions and dismissing his warnings as irrelevant.

At first sight Adam and Eve's failure to obey God may not appear especially heinous, but their actions have devastating consequences for humanity and the world. The impact of their actions is far reaching. They immediately become conscious of their nakedness and look to avoid God's presence. Their disobedience results in various punishments that splinter the harmony and unity of the Edenic environment. No longer may the human couple serve as God's vice-regents. By obeying a creature rather than the Creator, they have themselves become like the other creatures, a point driven home when they are clothed in animal skins (Gen. 3:21; cf. Rom. 1:18–32).

Adam and Eve's expulsion from the garden of Eden creates a major obstacle for the fulfillment of God's plan that he should dwell on earth with people who love and trust him. Something of this becomes evident in the episodes that immediately follow Genesis 3. As we shall observe in more detail in the next chapter, with their God-given capacity both to rule over others and to construct cities, humans separated from God fill the earth with violence and aspire to create a city that will enable them to access heaven itself.

Yet while the events recorded in Genesis 4–11 give a bleak picture of humanity's behavior and aspirations, God remains committed to his original creation plan. Amid the chaos that flows from Adam and Eve's betrayal, he graciously offers hope that someday humans will enjoy his intimate presence in an expanded garden of Eden. To this we shall return later.

1

The Godless City

With remarkable conciseness the opening chapters of Genesis introduce a story that looks forward to the creation of an exceptional city where God and humanity will live in harmony. Specific references to the city are muted, but the garden of Eden narrative sets the scene for what is to follow. Unexpectedly, however, the garden is invaded by a wily predator that deceives the human couple into disobeying their Creator. By submitting to the seductive prompting of the mysterious Serpent, Adam and Eve fail to fulfill their duty as God's vice-regents. Their authority to rule over the earth, delegated to them by God, passes to the Serpent (cf. Eph. 2:2). Consequently, they become subservient to it.

In view of God's aspirations for humanity, it is noteworthy that one of the activities associated with Cain is the building of a city. Genesis 4:17 states briefly: "Cain knew his wife, and she conceived and bore Enoch. When he built a city, he called the name of the city after the name of his son, Enoch." The Hebrew text does not say explicitly that Cain "built a city." Rather, it implies that he was building a city (cf. NIV). City building was in his DNA, a fact that is no surprise when we consider God's design for humanity. However, it is noteworthy that Cain names the city after his son, Enoch. By doing so he glorifies his own offspring rather than the One who has equipped him to be a city builder. Cain's actions anticipate the creation of further cities, but, as we shall see, this does not necessarily bode well for humanity.

References to city building do not figure prominently in Genesis 5–10. Rather, attention is given to how people fill the earth with violence (Gen. 6:13), resulting in God's punishing them by sending a flood. When Noah and his family emerge from the safety of the ark, God reaffirms to them the creation mandate to be fruitful and multiply and fill the earth (Gen. 9:1; cf. 9:7). This marks a new beginning for the earth, but, unfortunately, people continue to live in opposition to God.

Babel, the City of Pride

If God's intention in making the earth is the creation of a city, Genesis 11 introduces a short account that is highly ironic.

> Now the whole earth had one language and the same words. And as people migrated from the east, they found a plain in the land of Shinar and settled there. And they said to one another, "Come, let us make bricks, and burn them thoroughly." And they had brick for stone, and bitumen for mortar. Then they said, "Come, let us build ourselves a city and a tower with its top in the heavens, and let us make a name for ourselves, lest we be dispersed over the face of the whole earth." And the LORD came down to see the city and the tower, which the children of man had built. And the LORD said, "Behold, they are one people, and they have all one language, and this is only the beginning of what they will do. And nothing that

they propose to do will now be impossible for them. Come, let us go down and there confuse their language, so that they may not understand one another's speech." So the LORD dispersed them from there over the face of all the earth, and they left off building the city. Therefore its name was called Babel, because there the LORD confused the language of all the earth. And from there the LORD dispersed them over the face of all the earth. (Gen. 11:1–9)

This brief episode describes how humans set about building a city with a tower that will reach up to the heavens. They do this intentionally so that they will not be dispersed throughout the whole earth. This reverses the divine plan, for God is interested in making the whole earth his residence by filling it with holy people. In marked contrast, the people of Babel attempt to access heaven and avoid populating the earth. Babel epitomizes the antithesis of what God desires.

Although the Genesis 11 report of the building of Babel is exceptionally brief, nine verses in all, this city casts a long shadow over the whole of the Bible. It does so for a number of reasons. At the outset, Babel has to be viewed as the prototypical Godless city. In Babel we see people uniting as one to make a name for themselves by building a tower that reaches up to heaven itself. Their ambition is clearly motivated by pride in their ability to achieve great things. While in Genesis 3 Adam and Eve aspired to become like God, the inhabitants of Babel now seek to establish themselves as supreme not only on earth but in heaven as well. With incredible arrogance they attempt to build a tower that will enable them to take control of heaven itself. The building of Babel typifies two different characteristics of humanity: (a) the capacity of people to achieve great things; (b) the arrogance of those who have turned away from God.

What a wealth of human meanings converge in the single image of Babel! It is an ambivalent image, evoking powerful feelings of a wide range. On one side we can see the human longings for community, achievement, civilization, culture, technology, safety, security, permanence and fame. But countering these aspirations we sense the moral judgment against idolatry, pride, self-reliance, the urge of material power and the human illusion of infinite achievement.[1]

While in one sense the construction of Babel is a natural consequence of people using divinely given abilities, they do so without regard for the One who gifted them. Their aspirations are to replace God, not only on earth, but in heaven as well. Constructed by people for people alone, Babel is a mockery of what God intended when he created humans and commanded them to fill the earth. As we shall see, the phenomenon of Babel is not restricted to Genesis 11. Babel typifies every proud human enterprise that seeks to exalt the creature over the Creator.

Babel/Babylon

The use of "Babel" as the city's name in Genesis 11 is an anomaly. For centuries this city has been designated "Babel" in English. This name is derived from the Hebrew title for the city, *babel*. However, *babel*, which occurs over two hundred times in the Hebrew Bible, is almost always translated into English as "Babylon." Remarkably, in the whole of the Old Testament there are generally only two exceptions to this rule. These are Genesis 10:10 and 11:9, and even here a few English translations replace Babel in Genesis 10:10 with Babylon (e.g., NIV; JPS). Babel should be called Babylon.[2]

---

1. Anonymous, "Babel, Tower of," in *Dictionary of Biblical Imagery*, ed. L. Ryken, J. C. Wilhoit, and T. Longman (Downers Grove, IL: InterVarsity Press, 1998), 67.

2. As in HCSB.

When we name the city "Babylon," a highly significant pattern begins to emerge. Babel is not only the antithesis of the holy city that God desires to build upon the earth, but it is also its great rival and opponent. This is an especially significant theme, appearing in both Testaments. More shall be said about this later.

Babel/Babylon: The Kingdom of Nimrod

Babel/Babylon takes on added significance when we observe that the city is also associated with aggressive human leadership or kingship. This link may not appear very obvious, for Genesis 11:1–9 contains no reference to any king. However, Babel/Babylon is first mentioned in Genesis 10:8–12 in association with the powerful hunter Nimrod:

> Cush fathered Nimrod; he was the first on earth to be a mighty man. He was a mighty hunter before the LORD. Therefore it is said, "Like Nimrod a mighty hunter before the LORD." The beginning of his kingdom was Babel, Erech, Accad, and Calneh, in the land of Shinar. From that land he went into Assyria and built Nineveh, Rehoboth-Ir, Calah, and Resen between Nineveh and Calah; that is the great city.

Within Genesis 10 this passage stands apart. Verses 8–10 focus on Nimrod, about whom a few selected details are recorded. In most English versions, Nimrod is taken to be the subject of verse 11. However, it is more likely that verse 11 refers to the activity of Asshur, who founds cities in northern Mesopotamia.[3]

Nimrod is designated a powerful or mighty man, a hunter in the sight of the Lord. This description ought to be viewed negatively. While the Hebrew text may legitimately be translated in this context

---

3. Cf. KJV; NJB; NJPS. If the Hebrew name *'aššûr* denotes a person, and not a place, then Asshur is responsible for building a number of important cities, including Nineveh, Rehoboth-Ir, Calah, and Resen.

"in the sight of the Lord," it may also imply "against the Lord."[4] This latter sense seems more appropriate in the context of all that is said in Genesis 1–11. Nimrod's aggression as a person runs totally counter to what God intended when at creation he commissioned people to rule the earth on his behalf. His forceful nature recalls the violence of previous generations, who provoked God to anger.

Through the use of force, Nimrod founded an extensive kingdom that includes Babel/Babylon. He is also a role model for Asshur. Undoubtedly, this tradition of kingdom building through aggression lived on in these cities. Later in history, the inhabitants of both Babylon and Nineveh descended in destructive power on the kingdoms of Israel and Judah; the Assyrians destroyed the northern kingdom of Israel, and, at a different time, the Babylonians decimated the southern kingdom of Judah.

God intended humanity to rule over the earth in peace, but Nimrod uses power to establish a kingdom that is a distortion of the kingdom that God wants to create on the earth. By linking Nimrod to Babel/Babylon, the author of Genesis introduces the idea of two contrasting cities and kingdoms. Due to the rebellion of Adam and Eve, God's desire to establish his kingdom on the earth through the construction of a city is thwarted. Instead of ruling as his vice-regents, humans oppose God and establish alternative kingdoms.

Conclusion

When we grasp the true intention of the human city builders of Babel/Babylon, it is clear that their project is not as innocent as it may seem at first. On the contrary, what we have here is an account in which all the God-given abilities of humans are deliberately focused on creating a society that has no need of God. Confident in

---

4. Cf. Mary Katherine Hom, "'. . . A Mighty Hunter before YHWH': Genesis 10:9 and the Moral-Theological Evaluation of Nimrod," *VT* 60 (2010): 63–68.

their own capacity to meet every challenge, the inhabitants of Babel/ Babylon view the Creator as irrelevant. In light of God's initial creation project, the account of Genesis 11:1–9 is a stark reminder of how perverted human nature has become.

To hinder human aspiration to work together in opposition against the One who created them, God prevents people from understanding each other by introducing multiple languages. This leads to the creation of different ethnic groups and nations, who struggled to comprehend one another. Nevertheless, although God intervenes to halt the Babel/Babylon project by scattering the city's inhabitants throughout the earth, the human ambition to construct alternative, godless cities remains. Babel typifies every social enterprise that seeks to exalt the creature over the Creator. From Genesis to Revelation, Babel/Babylon features prominently as the symbol of humanity's attempt to govern themselves without reference to and in defiance of God.

In chapter 1 we explored the possibility that Genesis 1–2 introduces a story that anticipates the creation of an extraordinary city where God will dwell in harmony with humanity. Against this background, it is noteworthy that the last episode in the primeval era (Genesis 1–11) concerns the construction of a city. This metropolis, however, is the antithesis of what God desires. In the light of this, the rest of Genesis starts a process that will result in the creation of an alternative city where God will dwell on earth in harmony with people. In due course, God's actions will center on the city of Jerusalem, which will occupy center stage for much of the Old Testament and into the New Testament. But we have not heard the last of Babylon.

2

The Temple-City

Viewed with hindsight, the earliest chapters of Genesis anticipate the creation of a city where God and humanity will coexist in peace. However, tragedy strikes as Adam and Eve alienate themselves from God. Endowed with the necessary skills to be city builders, humans arrogantly attempt to accomplish what comes naturally to them without reference to God. Their actions lead to further alienation, as God fragments humanity into different ethnic groups and nations to restrain their godless ambitions. Against this background, God intervenes to establish a new human community that will ultimately inhabit the city of God.

Abraham: "Father" of a New Humanity

With the introduction of Abram (later renamed Abraham) a significant new development occurs in Genesis. Whereas the primeval era of Genesis 1–11 moves toward the creation of Babel/Babylon as a "Godless" city, with Abraham begins a process that will ultimately lead to the establishment of ancient Jerusalem as the city of God.

Abraham's earliest life is associated with the city of Ur in southern

Mesopotamia, close to the city of Babylon. From there, he and his family migrate to northern Mesopotamia, to the region of Paddan-aram. Responding to the Lord's call, Abraham leaves his family and migrates to the land of Canaan, accompanied by his wife, Sarah, and their nephew Lot. God's invitation to Abraham in Genesis 12:1–3 marks the beginning of a process that will see God coming to dwell on the earth.

Within the book of Genesis, God's call of Abraham is linked back to the building of Babel/Babylon in a noteworthy way. Abraham is deliberately contrasted with the people of Babel/Babylon. Whereas the inhabitants of Babel/Babylon aspire to make a name for themselves (Gen. 11:4), God promises in Genesis 12:2 to make Abraham's name great. With the divine promise that Abraham's descendants will become a great nation (Gen. 12:2), the expectation is created that they will participate in some way in the creation of the city where God will dwell in harmony with humanity. Moreover, God's words to Abraham climax in the suggestion that in God's plans Abraham will impact every family of the earth.

Writing centuries after the time of Abraham, the author of Hebrews highlights how the patriarchs of old anticipated the construction of God's city:

> By faith Abraham obeyed when he was called to go out to a place that he was to receive as an inheritance. And he went out, not knowing where he was going. By faith he went to live in the land of promise, as in a foreign land, living in tents with Isaac and Jacob, heirs with him of the same promise. For he was looking forward to the city that has foundations, whose designer and builder is God. By faith Sarah herself received power to conceive, even when she was past the age, since she considered him faithful who had promised. Therefore from

one man, and him as good as dead, were born descendants as many as the stars of heaven and as many as the innumerable grains of sand by the seashore. These all died in faith, not having received the things promised, but having seen them and greeted them from afar, and having acknowledged that they were strangers and exiles on the earth. For people who speak thus make it clear that they are seeking a homeland. If they had been thinking of that land from which they had gone out, they would have had opportunity to return. But as it is, they desire a better country, that is, a heavenly one. Therefore God is not ashamed to be called their God, for he has prepared for them a city. (Heb. 11:8–16)

These verses emphasize how Abraham looked forward in faith to the creation of a city designed and built by God. Alluding to this, the author of Hebrews exhorts his readers to have an identical hope. Moreover, he anticipates that he and they will join others to receive, together with the patriarchs, what God promised (Heb. 11:39–40). The author of Hebrews later describes this "city of the living God" as "the heavenly Jerusalem" (Heb. 12:22). Underlining his belief that the creation of this city is still to occur, the author of Hebrews states, "For here we have no lasting city, but we seek the city that is to come" (Heb. 13:14). Drawing heavily on Old Testament expectations, the author of Hebrews undoubtedly believes that one day he and others will live with God in a new Jerusalem.

In the patriarchal narratives of Genesis, a noteworthy recurring theme is the multiplication of Abraham's descendants. This undoubtedly picks up on the creation mandate that humans are to be fruitful and fill the earth. Within the patriarchal narratives, the theme of having numerous descendants is all the more striking because initially Abraham and Sarah are childless (Gen. 11:30). The same is also true for Abraham's immediate descendants, Isaac and Jacob, for their respective wives, Rebekah and Rachel, are also unable to have children (Gen. 25:21; 29:31). In spite of Abraham's childlessness, he receives divine promises assuring him that his descendants will be as numerous as the stars of the heavens (Gen. 15:5) and the sand of the seashore (Gen. 22:17). With good reason, much of the Abraham narrative concentrates on how God provides Abraham and Sarah with a son, Isaac, through whom various divine promises will begin to move toward fulfillment.

Alongside the promises associated with numerous descendants, the Genesis narrative also foreshadows the concept of God dwelling with humanity on the earth. In anticipation of the construction of the tabernacle as God's portable abode, Genesis records the existence of several sacrificial sites that were "impermanent, miniature forms of sanctuaries."[1] These sacred locations share certain features in common. First, God comes and makes himself known, addressing each patriarch with words that recall the creation mandate in Genesis 1:28 for humans to be fruitful and fill the earth.[2] Second, these theophanies are associated with altars that are often located on mountains.[3]

In light of the larger biblical narrative, it is highly significant that Abraham constructs an altar on Mount Moriah (Gen. 22:1–9), the location where later Solomon will build the temple in Jerusalem (2 Chron. 3:1). Acknowledging Abraham's obedience, the Lord guarantees through a divine oath that Abraham's descendants will be numerous and that one of Abraham's descendants will overcome his enemies and bring God's blessing to all the nations of the earth (Gen. 22:16–18).

---

1. G. K. Beale, "Eden, the Temple, and the Church's Mission in the New Creation," *JETS* 48 (2005): 14.
2. See Gen. 9:1, 7; 12:2–3; 17:2, 6, 8, 20; 22:17–18; 26:3–4, 24; 28:3–4; 35:11–12; cf. 41:52; 47:27; 48:4; 49:22.
3. See Gen. 8:20; 12:7–8; 13:4, 18; 22:9; 26:25; 33:20; 35:1, 3, 7.

The divine promises given to Abraham, and later to Isaac (Gen. 26:1–6), are repeated to Jacob during a nighttime vision.[4] Forced to flee for his life by his older twin brother, Esau, Jacob has a vision in which he witnesses a ladder or stairs connecting heaven and earth. In the vision, God addresses Jacob, promising him a safe return to the land of Canaan. Moreover, in spite of the fact that Jacob is fleeing alone, God promises him numerous descendants. The entire incident impacts Jacob so much that he names the location Bethel, "house of God" (Gen. 28:19). Years later, when Jacob returns from Paddan-aram to Canaan, God reappears to him and instructs him to reside at Bethel (Gen. 35:1–15). When Jacob subsequently builds an altar at Bethel, God speaks to him once more, reaffirming the promises that he had given previously (Gen. 35:11–12).

Toward the City of God

God's promises to the patriarchs include the expectation that their descendants will increase greatly in number. After their relocation to the land of Egypt, the Israelite population expands so much that the Egyptian pharaoh views them as a threat to the security of his kingdom. Strikingly, the book of Exodus briefly describes the growth of the Israelites: "But the people of Israel were fruitful and increased greatly; they multiplied and grew exceedingly strong, so that the land was filled with them" (Ex. 1:7). The concentration of verbs in this verse echoes closely the creation mandate in Genesis 1:28, where God instructs humans to be fruitful and multiply and fill the earth. The Hebrew term *'eretz*, translated "land" in Exodus 1:7, elsewhere is often translated "earth" (e.g., Gen. 1:28).

The opening verses of Exodus associate the growth of the Israelites with God's creation mandate for humanity. But they are soon

---

4. The divine promises of Gen. 28:13–15 echo those in Gen. 12:1–3; 22:16–18; 26:3–5.

enslaved by an Egyptian pharaoh, whose plans are diametrically opposed to those of God. While God intended humanity to build a city where he would dwell with them, the Egyptian king conscripts the Israelites to build store cities for his benefit. Pharaoh's opposition to God is all the more noteworthy when we recall that the Egyptian king was perceived by his subjects as being divine.

In light of how the Exodus story begins, God's deliverance of the Israelites from slavery to Pharaoh is significant. When the Israelites celebrate their remarkable deliverance from the Egyptian chariots at the Lake of Reeds,[5] their victory song of gratitude to the Lord ends by looking to the future. They sing:

> You will bring them in and plant them on your own
> > mountain,
> > the place, O LORD, which you have made for your
> > abode,
> > the sanctuary, O Lord, which your hands have
> > established.
> The LORD will reign forever and ever. (Ex. 15:17–18)

Freed from Egyptian oppression, the Israelites see themselves as starting on a journey that will end with them dwelling with God at a mountain location chosen by him. Prior to this, God had previously announced to Moses that the Israelites would go up out of Egypt to the land promised to the patriarchs, to the land of Canaan (Ex. 3:8, 17; 6:4, 8; 13:5). The expectation that they will dwell with God is very much in keeping with God's original creation plan.

Although progress is slow, after several centuries the Israelites eventually take full possession of the Promised Land. Under the leadership of King David, they finally capture the city of Jerusalem,

---

5. On the translation "Lake of Reeds" rather than "Red Sea," see T. Desmond Alexander, *Exodus*, ApOTC (London: Inter-Varsity Press, 2017), 195.

also known as Zion (2 Sam. 5:6–8). Soon afterward David brings to Jerusalem the ark of the covenant, a gold-plated chest that was viewed as the footstool of God's heavenly throne. As a result, Jerusalem becomes the center of God's kingdom on earth. When David subsequently desires to build a palace or temple for God in Jerusalem, God delegates the privilege of doing this to David's son Solomon (1 Kings 6–8).[6]

Replacing the portable tabernacle, the Jerusalem temple becomes the Lord's residence on earth. As Meyers observes:

> The very terminology used for the building ("house," "palace") and the emphasis on the extraordinary nature of its design and fabrication together provide symbolic statements that God is in residence on Zion. The furnishings meet the "needs" of the building's occupant, with the glory of those furnishings signifying the Glory within.[7]

Like the portable sanctuary, the temple constructed by Solomon has features that associate it with the garden of Eden. The temple is decorated with arboreal imagery, including carvings of lilies and pomegranates on the tops of pillars.[8]

After Solomon completes the building of the temple, God's presence fills it (1 Kings 8:10–11). Consequently, Jerusalem takes on a special significance as the place of God's earthly residence. By becoming the city of God, Jerusalem enjoys a unique status. As the author of Psalm 50 states: "Out of Zion, the perfection of beauty, / God shines forth" (Ps. 50:2).

---

6. The Hebrew noun *hêkāl* may be translated as either "palace" or "temple." In the ancient world a temple was considered to be a deity's palace.

7. Carol L. Meyers, "Temple, Jerusalem" *ABD*, ed. David Noel Freedman (New Haven, CT: Yale University Press, 1992), 6:360.

8. Mark S. Smith, *The Pilgrimage Pattern in Exodus*, JSOTSup 239 (Sheffield, UK: Sheffield Academic Press, 1997), 100, highlights this link between the temple and Eden.

Jerusalem: The City of God

Jerusalem is important as the location of God's earthly residence, which is reflected in the annual religious pilgrimages undertaken by the Israelites. Every pilgrimage offered an opportunity to draw near to God. In Psalm 84, the author captures well the joy of traveling to Jerusalem in order to enter the temple. He writes:

> How lovely is your dwelling place,
>   O Lord of hosts!
> My soul longs, yes, faints
>   for the courts of the Lord;
> my heart and flesh sing for joy
>   to the living God.
>
> Even the sparrow finds a home,
>   and the swallow a nest for herself,
>   where she may lay her young,
> at your altars, O Lord of hosts,
>   my King and my God.
> Blessed are those who dwell in your house,
>   ever singing your praise! *Selah*
>
> Blessed are those whose strength is in you,
>   in whose heart are the highways to Zion. (Ps. 84:1–5)

Pilgrimages to Jerusalem were special occasions, offering ancient Israelites an opportunity to come near the Lord. The significance of these regular visits to the Jerusalem temple is noted by Smith:

> In sum, the pilgrimage was like visiting paradise and temporarily recapturing the primordial peaceful and abundant relationship with God. It involved both holiness and pleasure, sacred and aesthetic space. It was an experience imbued

with holiness, the beauty of the divine dwelling, and the very presence of God. The pilgrims' experience in the Temple was global in its effects. It saturated the psalmists' senses with all kinds of wonders: abundant food and incense, music and singing, gold and silver, palm trees, water and cherubs. This joyful experience led further to an experience of awe and holiness in the presence of God.[9]

The importance of pilgrimages to worship in Jerusalem explains why an entire section of the Psalter is devoted to songs used by pilgrims ascending to the temple on Mount Zion. The Songs of Ascent, Psalms 120–134, reflect and shape the thinking of those who travel to Jerusalem in order to draw closer to God. As Psalm 122 states, "I was glad when they said to me, / 'Let us go to the house of the LORD!' / Our feet have been standing / within your gates, O Jerusalem!" (vv. 1–2). These journeys to Jerusalem, which were repeated on a regular basis, may have intensified the Israelites' hope of living eternally in God's presence.

In keeping with this emphasis upon Jerusalem as God's earthly dwelling place, Psalm 87 highlights the privilege of being counted as a citizen of Jerusalem:

On the holy mount stands the city he founded;
 the LORD loves the gates of Zion
 more than all the dwelling places of Jacob.
Glorious things of you are spoken,
 O city of God. *Selah*

Among those who know me I mention Rahab and
  Babylon;
 behold, Philistia and Tyre, with Cush—

---

9. Ibid., 109.

"This one was born there," they say.
And of Zion it shall be said,
    "This one and that one were born in her";
    for the Most High himself will establish her.
The Lord records as he registers the peoples,
    "This one was born there." *Selah*

Singers and dancers alike say,
    "All my springs are in you." (Ps. 87:1–7)

Everyone dwelling in Zion is blessed because of God's presence, a theme echoed elsewhere in the Psalter (e.g., Ps. 133:1–3; 147:12–14). As the author of Psalm 84 affirms:

For a day in your courts is better
    than a thousand elsewhere.
I would rather be a doorkeeper in the house of my God
    than dwell in the tents of wickedness.
For the Lord God is a sun and shield;
    the Lord bestows favor and honor.
No good thing does he withhold
    from those who walk uprightly.
O Lord of hosts,
    blessed is the one who trusts in you! (Ps. 84:10–12)

The hope generated by the concept of the temple-city permeated the thinking of Israelites. Life in God's presence promised personal well-being and security, as God lavishes his love upon those known to him. With profound delight, the author of Psalm 27 anticipates the glorious experience of dwelling in the house of God. He writes, "One thing have I asked of the Lord, / that will I seek after: / that I may dwell in the house of the Lord / all the days of my life, / to gaze upon the beauty of the Lord / and to inquire in his temple" (Ps. 27:4). The author of Psalm 23 conveys a similar hope:

The Lord is my shepherd; I shall not want.
    He makes me lie down in green pastures.
He leads me beside still waters.
    He restores my soul.
He leads me in paths of righteousness
    for his name's sake.

Even though I walk through the valley of the shadow of death,
    I will fear no evil,
for you are with me;
    your rod and your staff,
    they comfort me.

You prepare a table before me
    in the presence of my enemies;
you anoint my head with oil;
    my cup overflows.
Surely goodness and mercy shall follow me
    all the days of my life,
and I shall dwell in the house of the Lord
    forever. (Ps. 23:1–6)

While we might interpret their hopes as referring merely to their experience of going to the temple in Jerusalem, there is good reason to think that these hopes anticipate an experience that lies beyond this life. How else could the psalmist expect to dwell in God's house "forever" (Ps. 23:6)?[10]

---

10. For a fuller treatment of how a desire to dwell with God permeates the Psalter, see Jerome F. D. Creach, *The Destiny of the Righteous in the Psalms* (St. Louis, MO: Chalice Press, 2008), 124–34.

Conclusion

The establishment of Jerusalem as the city of God was an important development toward the fulfillment of God's creation plan to establish a city that would fill the whole earth. Yet while ancient Jerusalem exemplified in part what God intended for the whole world, it was not the final product.

The history of Israelite Jerusalem is not a straightforward story of divine presence and blessing. The fortunes of the city rise and fall. Eventually, ancient Jerusalem was destroyed by the Babylonians, a noteworthy "coincidence" in light of Genesis 11:1–9. But before we explore the fall of Jerusalem and its implications, there are two other significant features of the temple-city that need to be explored. The first of these concerns its portrayal as a holy mountain; this will be examined in the next chapter. The second concerns its function as a royal city, the capital of the kingdom of God under the rule of a divinely appointed human dynasty; this will be considered in chapter 5.

3

The Holy Mountain City

The concept of Jerusalem as a temple-city fits appropriately with the expectation that God created the earth to be his dwelling place. Intimately linked to the concept of temple-city is the idea that God's residence will be located on a holy hill or mountain. The importance of Jerusalem as a mountain location is conveyed by the designation "Mount Zion," which is often used as a synonym for Jerusalem.

Many Old Testament passages portray Jerusalem as a holy mountain. The opening section of Psalm 48 provides one of the most memorable illustrations of this:

> Great is the LORD and greatly to be praised
>   in the city of our God!
> His holy mountain, beautiful in elevation,
>   is the joy of all the earth,
> Mount Zion, in the far north,
>   the city of the great King. (Ps. 48:1–2)

This psalm, however, is not alone in appreciating the significance of God dwelling on a holy mountain. A very similar affirmation, linking the concepts of holy mountain, city, and the divine abode, comes at the start of Psalm 87:

> A Psalm of the Sons of Korah. A Song.
>
>> On the holy mount stands the city he founded;
>>> the LORD loves the gates of Zion
>> more than all the dwelling places of Jacob.
>> Glorious things of you are spoken,
>>> O city of God. *Selah* (Ps. 87:1–3)

Here, the city of God is clearly linked to a holy Mount Zion. In Psalm 43, the author expresses a strong desire to come to God's holy hill, to his "dwelling," so that he may approach the "altar of God" in order to praise him with the lyre (vv. 3–4; cf. 2:6; 3:4; 15:1; 24:3; 99:9). While not specifically mentioning a hill or a mountain in every psalm, the Songs of Ascent,[1] grouped together as Psalms 120–134, also draw attention to God dwelling on a holy mountain.[2]

Outside of the Psalter, the prophet Isaiah frequently links God's presence to a mountain location. He does so especially when speaking about the future transformation of Jerusalem "in the latter days":

> It shall come to pass in the latter days
>> that the mountain of the house of the LORD
> shall be established as the highest of the mountains,
>> and shall be lifted up above the hills;
> and all the nations shall flow to it,
>> and many peoples shall come, and say:
> "Come, let us go up to the mountain of the LORD,
>> to the house of the God of Jacob,

---

1. These were sung by worshipers ascending the road to Jerusalem.
2. For a fuller survey of Mount Zion in the Psalter, see Jerome F. D. Creach, *The Destiny of the Righteous in the Psalms* (St. Louis, MO: Chalice Press, 2008), 111–23.

that he may teach us his ways
> and that we may walk in his paths." (Isa. 2:2–3; cf.
>> Mic. 4:1–2)

By predicting that "the mountain of the house of the LORD" will become "the highest of the mountains," Isaiah anticipates a time when God's sovereignty over all the earth will be fully acknowledged by all the nations. As Gowan remarks, "This is a theological, not a topographical, statement."[3] Isaiah's use of mountain imagery underlines that God himself will be exalted in majesty as he exercises supreme authority over the whole earth. This expectation anticipates the fulfillment of God's creation blueprint, for Isaiah envisages the Lord dwelling in a city that will fill the world.[4]

The prophet Ezekiel is also conscious of the concept of a mountain city where God dwells (e.g., Ezek. 20:40). While in the early part of his prophetic ministry he witnesses God's departure from Jerusalem, his final vision in chapters 40–48 is of a restored temple-city. Interestingly, he introduces this material with these words:

> In visions of God he brought me to the land of Israel, and set me down on a very high mountain, on which was a structure like a city to the south. (Ezek. 40:2)

Another example of mountain imagery comes in the postexilic book of Zechariah. In chapter 8 Zechariah reports the Lord's words concerning his return to Jerusalem:

> Thus says the LORD: I have returned to Zion and will dwell in the midst of Jerusalem, and Jerusalem shall be called the faithful city, and the mountain of the LORD of hosts, the holy mountain. (Zech. 8:3)

---

3. Donald E. Gowan, *Eschatology in the Old Testament* (Philadelphia: Fortress Press, 1986), 11.
4. For more on this, see chap. 6, "Envisaging a Transformed Jerusalem."

Once more we witness a convergence of the concepts of city, holy mountain, and God's abode, paralleling closely Exodus 15:17.

In light of the prominence given to God's living on a holy mountain, it is worth observing that the kingdom of God is associated with a mountain in Daniel 2. The contents of the chapter center on a dream that involves a huge statue made of different materials. Eventually, Daniel interprets this dream for King Nebuchadnezzar, a Babylonian:

> You saw, O king, and behold, a great image. This image, mighty and of exceeding brightness, stood before you, and its appearance was frightening. The head of this image was of fine gold, its chest and arms of silver, its middle and thighs of bronze, its legs of iron, its feet partly of iron and partly of clay. As you looked, a stone was cut out by no human hand, and it struck the image on its feet of iron and clay, and broke them in pieces. Then the iron, the clay, the bronze, the silver, and the gold, all together were broken in pieces, and became like the chaff of the summer threshing floors; and the wind carried them away, so that not a trace of them could be found. But the stone that struck the image became a great mountain and filled the whole earth. (Dan. 2:31–35)

From the surrounding context it is evident that the stone that strikes the image symbolizes the kingdom of God. In light of other passages that associate God's dwelling place with a mountain, it is understandable that his kingdom should be portrayed as a great mountain that fills the whole earth. To the former citizens of Jerusalem now in exile, Nebuchadnezzar's dream foretells the future demise of Babylon and of other human kingdoms opposed to God. All of these will one day be replaced by God's kingdom.

The Mountain of God at Sinai

In assessing the origin of the holy mountain-city tradition associated with Jerusalem/Zion, scholars have tended in recent years to favor the idea that this was taken over from the Canaanites, who shared with other ancient Near Eastern peoples a belief in a cosmic mountain.[5] While it is true that some features associated with the cosmic mountain concept, but by no means all, are found in biblical texts concerning Jerusalem/Mount Zion, it is much more likely that the concept of a holy mountain is derived from the exodus-Sinai experience of the Israelites. This provides a much better explanation for the origin of the mountain concept, especially with its emphasis on the holy nature of the location. Unfortunately, Old Testament scholarship has tended to conceive of the traditions linked to Sinai and Zion as promoting very different, if not opposing, aspirations.[6]

Of all the events described in the Old Testament, the Israelites' dramatic rescue from Egypt and their subsequent encounter with God at Mount Sinai stand apart. This sequence of events, which comprises the heart of the Pentateuch, is narrated in the books of Exodus, Leviticus, and Numbers. The importance of the exodus-Sinai experience is underlined by the very detailed description of what took place. Reporting events that occurred over a period of about twenty-four months, no other era of Israelite history is documented so fully. The Israelites' experience had a long-lasting impact upon the nation, being memorialized in a variety of ways.

God's rescue of the Israelites from Egypt and his encounter with them at Mount Sinai is an integral part of a much larger

---

5. Richard J. Clifford, *The Cosmic Mountain in Canaan and the Old Testament*, HSM 4 (Cambridge, MA: Harvard University Press, 1972).

6. For examples, see B. C. Ollenburger, *Zion, City of the Great King: A Theological Symbol of the Jerusalem Cult*, JSOTSup 41 (Sheffield, UK: JSOT Press, 1987), 151–55.

program designed to facilitate God and people dwelling together in harmony on the earth. This outcome is noted briefly in the victory song of the Israelites in Exodus 15, which celebrates their dramatic deliverance from Pharaoh's chariot force at the Lake of Reeds. The first part of this triumph song recalls what God has already done for them, but the final stanzas look to the future.[7] In doing so, verse 17 anticipates the people dwelling with God. The Israelites sing to the Lord: "You will bring them in and plant them on your own mountain, / the place, O Lᴏʀᴅ, which you have made for your abode, / the sanctuary, O Lord, which your hands have established" (Ex. 15:17). These words, probably composed by the prophetess Miriam, Moses's sister, refer to the place that God has made for his abode.[8]

Two significant features of this future abode are mentioned here. First, it is situated on a mountain. Second, it is designated a "sanctuary." This latter term implies that it is a holy location, for the Hebrew noun *miqdāš*, which means "holy place," is used elsewhere to denote the tabernacle (e.g., Ex. 25:8; Lev. 16:33) and the temple (e.g., 1 Chron. 22:19; Ezek. 37:28). Looking to the future, the Israelites envisage living with God on his holy mountain. This is where the city of God will be constructed.

For the Israelites, freed from bondage to Pharaoh, their journey to the Promised Land is not merely about finding an alternative country where they may dwell. As anticipated in the patriarchal narratives, the Israelites have reason to believe that they will dwell on God's holy mountain.[9] The hope proclaimed in Exodus 15:17 is based on prior expectations.

---

7. On the structure of the song, especially regarding v. 13, see T. Desmond Alexander, *Exodus*, ApOTC (London: Inter-Varsity Press, 2017), 301–3.

8. For Miriam being the author of the song, see T. Desmond Alexander, *Exodus*, Teach the Text (Grand Rapids, MI: Baker, 2016), 72.

9. See chap. 3.

If the final destination of the Israelites is a mountain city that God has prepared as his dwelling place, it is especially noteworthy that on their trek to this mountain abode God brings his redeemed people to another mountain. But this is no ordinary mountain. When this mountain is first introduced in the Exodus narrative, it is intentionally designated "the mountain of God" (Ex. 3:1). It is here that Moses first encounters God. Located in the region of Horeb, only later is this mountain specifically called Mount Sinai (Ex. 19:11).[10]

The events associated with Mount Sinai are exceptionally important, for they anticipate and prepare for the time when God will live with the Israelites on Mount Zion/Jerusalem.[11] In doing so, the books of Exodus and Leviticus give particular attention to the topic of holiness, recognizing that for the Israelites to dwell with God on his holy mountain, they too need to be holy.

As we shall observe in more detail below, the book of Exodus sheds vital light on the process by which humans, alienated from God, may be sanctified in order to come into his holy presence. Leviticus consolidates and expands on this by revealing what is required in order to be a holy nation. In essence, Exodus and Leviticus record how God orientates the Israelites toward holy living, an essential requirement for all citizens of the city of God.

Exodus begins by describing how the Israelites are enslaved by tyrannical pharaohs, who prevent them from fulfilling God's creation mandate. In large measure, chapters 1–15 record how God rescues his enslaved people from the control of evil rulers, who consider themselves to be gods. God's deliverance of the Israelite slaves may be viewed as an act of redemption, a familiar

---

10. Mount Sinai lies within the region of Horeb. See Alexander, *Exodus*, 81–82.
11. Ex. 15:17 does not specify the location of the holy mountain. This becomes known only much later.

concept in the ancient world, where slavery was ubiquitous. The concept of redemption is mentioned briefly in Exodus 6:6, where God promises to redeem the Israelites "with an outstretched arm and with great acts of judgment." Later, in Exodus 15:13, the Israelites describe themselves as the people whom the Lord has redeemed. In both these passages, the Hebrew verb used is *gā'al*, from which is derived the term *gō'ēl*, "kinsman-redeemer" (cf. Ruth 3:9; 4:1 NIV). In rescuing the Israelites from slavery, God comes as a relative—in Exodus 4:22 he describes Israel as his firstborn son—to redeem those who are being unjustly exploited. This redemption from evil powers represents a necessary first stage in the process by which the Israelites will be enabled to live in God's presence.

Mount Sinai and Holiness

Redemption alone, however, is not sufficient to make the Israelites holy. By nature, people are sinful and unclean. For this reason, when the Israelites arrive at Mount Sinai, they are strongly prohibited from ascending the mountain of God; they have not yet been consecrated/sanctified. Because they are not holy, God instructs Moses to warn the people: "Take care not to go up into the mountain or touch the edge of it. Whoever touches the mountain shall be put to death. No hand shall touch him, but he shall be stoned or shot; whether beast or man, he shall not live" (Ex. 19:12–13). To underline the severity of this prohibition God later cautions Moses that even the priests must not ascend the mountain (Ex. 19:21–24). Until the people are properly sanctified, access to God's presence is prohibited; only Moses is permitted to go up the mountain.

Against this background, the events of Exodus 24 are significant. After a covenant ratification ritual that involves the offering of two types of sacrifices and the sprinkling of blood, prominent representatives of the Israelites safely ascend the lower part of Mount Sinai:

> Then Moses and Aaron, Nadab, and Abihu, and seventy of the elders of Israel went up, and they saw the God of Israel. There was under his feet as it were a pavement of sapphire stone, like the very heaven for clearness. And he did not lay his hand on the chief men of the people of Israel; they beheld God, and ate and drank. (Ex. 24:9–11)

In this short but remarkable passage, some of the Israelites witness God's glory in a more intimate way than had previously been possible. At Mount Sinai some Israelite elders get a glimpse in anticipation of what will ultimately be the city of God. Their experience is a foretaste of something much better to come.

After the Lord establishes a unique covenant relationship with the Israelites, the way is prepared for him to come and dwell in their midst. For this to become a reality, God instructs Moses to construct a resplendent, portable sanctuary (often known as the tabernacle). Once the manufacturing instructions, which are given in considerable detail (Exodus 25–31), are fully implemented (Exodus 35–39), the sanctuary is erected (Exodus 40). God then comes to dwell within it (Ex. 40:34).

The portable sanctuary consists of an outer courtyard and a tent divided into two compartments. While much could be said about it, for present purposes it is sufficient to note that the sanctuary is deliberately designed to resemble Mount Sinai. Drawing on a longstanding Jewish tradition, Sarna writes:

> During the theophany, the mount was separated into three distinct zones of increasing degrees of holiness and re-

striction of access. At the foot of the mount stood the people, and there the altar was set up; in like manner, the altar was placed in the Court of the Tabernacle to which the laity had access. Higher up on the mount was the second zone of holiness, to which only the priests and elders were admitted. Corresponding to this in the Tabernacle was the Holy Place, which was restricted to the priesthood. The summit of the mountain constituted the third zone, which was exclusively reserved for Moses. Its counterpart in the Tabernacle was the Holy of Holies. Just as the Lord communicated with Moses on the mountaintop, so He does in the Holy of Holies; and in the same way that the cloud covered Mount Sinai after Moses had ascended, so the Tabernacle became enveloped in cloud on its completion, and the pillar of fire hovered over both Sinai and it.[12]

These observations provide a secure basis for believing that the portable sanctuary is intentionally modeled on Mount Sinai. Noting close verbal parallels between Exodus 24:15b–16a; 18a; 25:1–2a and 40:34–Leviticus 1:2, Averbeck observes, "The tabernacle became the medium through which the Lord in his true presence traveled from the mountain of God (Sinai) to accompany and guide Israel from there to the Promised Land. The tabernacle was, therefore, a sort of movable Sinai."[13] The "mountain of God" goes with the people as they journey to the Promised Land. This best explains why Mount Sinai never becomes a sacred location and a place of pilgrimage.

---

12. Nahum M. Sarna, *Exploring Exodus: The Origins of Biblical Israel* (New York: Schocken, 1996), 203.

13. "Tabernacle," in *Dictionary of the Old Testament: Pentateuch*, ed. T. D. Alexander and D. W. Baker (Downers Grove, IL: InterVarsity Press, 2003), 824.

SIMILARITIES BETWEEN MOUNT SINAI AND THE PORTABLE SANCTUARY

MOUNT SINAI

TABERNACLE

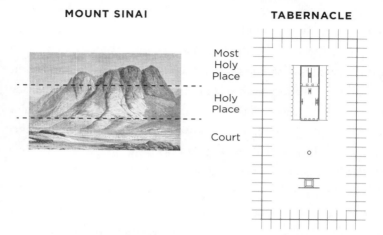

Most Holy Place

Holy Place

Court

Tabernacle illustration adapted from "The Tabernacle and Court," in *ESV Study Bible*, ed. Wayne Grudem (Wheaton, IL: Crossway, 2008), 190–91.

The link between Mount Sinai and the portable sanctuary is highly significant; it enables the Israelites symbolically to transport "the mountain of God" to the Promised Land. Consequently, "the tabernacle becomes an important way of carrying the Sinai experience forward during the subsequent wanderings."[14] Moreover, the rituals associated with Mount Sinai become a regular feature of Israelite worship at the portable sanctuary and much later at the temple in the city of Jerusalem. As Childs briefly notes, "What happened at Sinai is continued in the tabernacle."[15] Reflecting this idea, but from a later perspective when Jerusalem/Zion is viewed as the "mountain of God," Lundquist remarks, "These conceptions of Zion as a holy mountain go back ultimately to the inner-Israelite experience at Sinai. The temple of

---

14. Göran Larsson, *Bound for Freedom: The Book of Exodus in Jewish and Christian Traditions* (Peabody, MA: Hendrickson, 1999), 134.

15. Brevard S. Childs, *The Book of Exodus: A Critical, Theological Commentary*, OTL (London: SCM, 1974), 540.

Solomon would seem ultimately to be little more than the architectural realization and the ritual enlargement of the Sinai experience."[16]

Thus far we have observed how God brings the Israelites to Mount Sinai in anticipation of planting them on his holy mountain in the Promised Land. Before the Israelites can ascend the "mountain of God" they must first enter into a friendship treaty with him and be consecrated. The importance of this latter process is underlined when we note the correspondence between Mount Sinai and the portable sanctuary. Close parallels exist between the consecration ritual that enables the Israelite elders to ascend the lower part of Mount Sinai (Ex. 24:3–11) and the process by which the Levitical priests are sanctified in order to serve within the portable sanctuary (Ex. 29:1–37). To ascend the mountain or enter the sanctuary people need to be made holy. This is a prerequisite for those who will dwell in God's holy city.

Degrees of Holiness and Uncleanness

Before exploring these corresponding rituals associated with consecration/sanctification, it is important to understand something of the cultural context in which they took place. For the ancient Israelites their world was dominated by four significant categories (holy and common, clean and unclean). The importance of these categories is underlined by the fact that God instructed the priests "to distinguish between the holy and the common, and between the unclean and the clean" (Lev. 10:10). Apart from the Hebrew term *ḥōl*, "common,"[17] which comes in Leviticus only in this verse, the concepts of holy, clean, and unclean are frequently mentioned in Leviticus.[18]

---

16. John M. Lundquist, "What Is a Temple? A Preliminary Typology," in *The Quest for the Kingdom of God: Studies in Honor of George E. Mendenhall*, ed. H. B. Huffmon, F. A. Spina, and A. R. W. Green (Winona Lake, IN: Eisenbrauns, 1983), 207.

17. The term *ḥōl* would appear to designate everything that is not holy.

18. Terms based on the Hebrew root *qādaš* (e.g., *holy, holiness, sanctify*) come 152 times in Leviticus; this represents about one-fifth of all occurrences in the OT. The adjective *ṭāhôr*, "clean/pure," and associated terms occur seventy-four times in Leviticus; this accounts for more than

Holiness is intimately linked to God, for he alone is innately holy. Moreover, holiness emanates from God. For this reason, everything that comes close to God is made holy. We witness this at Mount Sinai, for God's presence sanctifies the mountain.[19] The further away something is from God, the less holy it is. Eventually, there is a boundary between holy and common; in the case of the portable sanctuary this boundary is marked by the curtained fence that surrounds the enclosure. Everything outside the curtained enclosure is common.

The distinction between holy and common is important, but we should also observe that there are differing degrees of holiness. We see this with both Mount Sinai and the portable sanctuary. The portable sanctuary consists of three distinctive regions. The tent is comprised of two rooms, the Most Holy Place (or Holy of Holies) and the Holy Place. The Most Holy Place, as its name suggests, has the highest degree of holiness. Here God dwells, his feet resting on the ark of the covenant, the footstool of his heavenly throne.[20] Separated by a curtain from the Most Holy Place is the Holy Place, which contains the golden incense altar, the lampstand, and the table for the bread of the Presence.

The Holy Place has a less intense level of holiness. The courtyard of the portable sanctuary is also considered holy, but to a lesser degree. The different levels of holiness associated with the different parts of the portable sanctuary are reflected in a variety of ways, including the type and quality of the materials used in the construction of each area and in the access that people have to each part. Access to the courtyard is available to all Israelites who are deemed clean. Priests may enter the Holy Place, but only the high priest may enter the Most Holy Place.

---

one-third of all OT occurrences. The adjective *ṭāmē'*, "unclean," and cognate terms come 132 times in Leviticus; this represents more than half of all occurrences in the OT. These statistics underscore the importance of these categories within the Sinai narrative.

19. Moses first encounters God at Mount Sinai when herding his flock. Ex. 3:5 records that Moses had to remove his sandals because the ground was holy.

20. See 1 Chron. 28:2; cf. Pss. 99:5; 132:7.

Whereas holiness is associated with God, uncleanness represents the antithesis of everything holy. As there are different intensities of holiness, there are different degrees of uncleanness. This is reflected in the regulations recorded in Leviticus. For example, a person becomes unclean by touching an animal carcass. However, the level of uncleanness is intensified if the person carries the carcass. Anyone carrying a carcass has to wash his or her clothes in order to attain ritual purity again. Washing of clothes is not necessary for someone who merely touches a carcass; such a person, however, remains unclean until the evening (Lev. 11:24–28).

The categories of holy, clean, and unclean were exceptionally important for the ancient Israelites, especially when God, the Holy One, lived in their midst.[21] By observing what distinguished one degree of uncleanness or holiness from another, the Israelites were enabled to comprehend the nature of ultimate holiness. As they moved from one level of holiness to a higher level, there was a greater intensity in terms of perfection, purity, righteousness, and love. Ultimately, to be in God's presence demanded the highest level of holiness possible. Only those who have the highest degree of holiness can inhabit the city of God.

INCREASING HOLINESS

greater purity
greater perfection
greater wholeness
greater love

---

21. For more on the different levels of holiness, see T. Desmond Alexander, *From Paradise to the Promised Land: An Introduction to the Pentateuch*, 3rd ed. (Grand Rapids, MI: Baker, 2012), 237–48.

The Process of Consecration

Not only does Leviticus establish boundaries between different degrees of holiness and uncleanness, but very importantly it describes rituals that enable people to move from one degree of uncleanness or holiness to another. These rituals are associated with cleansing and atonement. This is illustrated, for example, in the process by which a man who has become unclean due to a bodily discharge is made clean again:

> And when the one with a discharge is cleansed of his discharge, then he shall count for himself seven days for his cleansing, and wash his clothes. And he shall bathe his body in fresh water and shall be clean. And on the eighth day he shall take two turtledoves or two pigeons and come before the LORD to the entrance of the tent of meeting and give them to the priest. And the priest shall use them, one for a sin offering and the other for a burnt offering. And the priest shall make atonement for him before the LORD for his discharge. (Lev. 15:13–15)

Of the various consecration rituals recorded in Exodus and Leviticus, the most detailed involves the consecration of the Aaronic priests. Since Aaron and his sons are privileged with serving inside the portable sanctuary, it is essential for them to be made holy in order that they may come close to God in safety. Instructions for their consecration are recorded in Exodus 29:1–37. The implementation of these instructions is reported in Leviticus 8:1–36. These rituals illustrate how those who desire to dwell in the city of God can be cleansed and made holy.

The initial consecration ritual for the priests involves a series of activities, which are repeated daily for seven days. At the outset

Aaron and his sons are washed with water (Lev. 8:5) and then anointed with oil (Lev. 8:12). After this, a bull is sacrificed as a sin (or purification) offering in order to purify the bronze altar located immediately outside the entrance to the tent (Lev. 8:14–17). A ram is then offered as a whole burnt offering, the entire animal being consumed by fire on the altar (Lev. 8:18–21). This offering functions as a ransom, the life of the ram being a substitute for the lives of Aaron and his sons. A second ram is also offered as a sacrifice (Lev. 8:22).[22] On this occasion only some parts of the ram are burnt upon the altar. Some of its blood is daubed on the lobe of Aaron's right ear, on the thumb of his right hand, and on the big toe of his right foot (Lev. 8:23). The same process is repeated for Aaron's sons (Lev. 8:24). This is intended to cleanse Aaron and his sons from defilement. The remaining blood is then thrown against the sides of the bronze altar; this makes the blood holy. After this, certain parts of the ram that have not been burnt on the altar are given to Aaron (Lev. 8:25–27). Next, some anointing oil and some of the holy blood from the altar are sprinkled on Aaron and his garments and on his sons and their garments (Lev. 8:30). When this holy blood touches Aaron and his sons, they become holy.

Finally, Aaron and his sons are required to eat the sacrificial meat (Lev. 8:31–32). This complex ritual, which atones for their sin, is repeated for seven days (Lev. 8:33), indicating that the highest level of holiness cannot be easily obtained. The length of this process reflects the higher degree of holiness required in order to serve in the portable sanctuary. Without the provision of appropriate sacrifices to cleanse or purify those who are defiled, ransom them from the domain of death, and impart to them a holy status, Aaron and his sons could not approach the Holy One.

---

22. This offering resembles the peace (or fellowship) offering.

In light of the correspondence between Mount Sinai and the portable sanctuary, it is not surprising that the process for consecrating Aaron and his sons has certain similarities with the ritual used to consecrate the Israelites when the covenant is sealed. An altar stands at the entrance to the tabernacle, corresponding to the altar that stood at the foot of the mountain.[23] Fewer details are provided in Exodus 24, and no sin (or purification) offering is made to sanctify the temporary altar built of stones. However, whole burnt offerings and peace (or fellowship) offerings are made at the sealing of the covenant.

Strikingly, the Passover ritual has features similar to those of the covenant ratification ceremony and the consecration of the priests. At Passover, a ransom is paid for the lives of the firstborn males, the homes of the Israelites are purified by the sprinkling of blood on the doorframes, and the people eat sacrificial or holy food.[24] A consequence of Passover is that all the firstborn males now belong to God (Ex. 13:12). Later, through another ransom payment, the tribe of Levi becomes a substitute for the firstborn males of all the other tribes (Num. 3:12–13). Consequently, the Levites have the privilege of being more closely associated with the portable sanctuary than other Israelite tribes.

Since God's ultimate intention is that the Israelites should live with him on his holy mountain, it is essential that they should become holy. The consecration rituals encountered in Exodus and Leviticus are an important reminder that sinful people may ascend the mountain of God and become citizens of the city of God only after they have been sanctified. Holiness, which embraces moral purity

---

23. The golden incense altar within the Holy Place is viewed as replicating the bronze altar outside the tent. When the priests offer the morning and evening sacrifices on the bronze altar, the high priest offers incense upon the golden altar.

24. See T. Desmond Alexander, "The Passover Sacrifice," in *Sacrifice in the Bible*, ed. R. T. Beckwith and M. Selman (Grand Rapids, MI: Baker, 1995), 1–24.

and perfection, is unattainable but for the grace of God. He is the One who redeems sinful people from the power of evil, ransoms them from the domain of death, and makes them holy. As God reminds the Israelites, "I am the LORD who sanctifies you" (Lev. 20:8; 22:32; cf. 21:15, 23; 22:9, 16).

While the regulations of Leviticus draw attention to God's gracious provision of consecration rituals, the Israelites are also expected to fulfill their calling as God's people. They must live holy lives. Not surprisingly, God instructs them: "You shall be holy, for I the LORD your God am holy" (Lev. 19:2; cf. 11:44–45; 20:26). The moral implications of this are highlighted especially in Leviticus 18–20, where integrity, sexual purity, and love of others are emphasized alongside other virtues. Holiness is not about being especially pious; it is about caring for the childless, the poor, and the refugee.

The Levitical instructions address a particular time in history and are set in a particular location. Although the requirement to be holy in order to live in God's presence is universal and eternal, the Sinai covenant, the tabernacle, and the Levitical priesthood are all temporary in nature. The regulations of Leviticus are not intended to last forever, for they presuppose an environment that is still dominated by sin, uncleanness, and death. They point toward something more permanent; they anticipate life in the holy city of God.

Dwelling on the Holy Mountain of God

We began this chapter by observing some of the biblical references to Jerusalem/Mount Zion as the holy mountain where God resides. We have subsequently observed that the concept of "holy mountain" lies at the heart of the exodus-Sinai experience. In the book of Psalms, further evidence is readily available to support the Sinai-Zion connection.

Adopting striking imagery, the author of Psalm 68 highlights the concept of God's mountain abode by addressing one of the mountains of Bashan: "Why do you look with hatred, O many-peaked mountain, / at the mount that God desired for his abode, / yes, where the LORD will dwell forever" (v. 16)? The inspired poet then proceeds to emphasize the Lord's tremendous power, before unexpectedly remarking, "Sinai is now in the sanctuary" (v. 17). This unusual comment is probably best explained by recalling how the portable sanctuary, constructed at Mount Sinai, functions as a model of the mountain. Consequently, Mount Sinai was closely associated with the Lord's sanctuary on Mount Zion.

The author of Psalm 15 begins his song by asking God: "O LORD, who shall sojourn in your tent? / Who shall dwell on your holy hill?" (v. 1). These questions recall the requirement to be holy in order to ascend Mount Sinai. In light of this, the contents of Psalm 15 resonate with the covenant obligations set out in the Decalogue and the Book of the Covenant:

> He who walks blamelessly and does what is right
> and speaks truth in his heart;
> who does not slander with his tongue
> and does no evil to his neighbor,
> nor takes up a reproach against his friend;
> in whose eyes a vile person is despised,
> but who honors those who fear the LORD;
> who swears to his own hurt and does not change;
> who does not put out his money at interest
> and does not take a bribe against the innocent.
> He who does these things shall never be moved. (Ps. 15:2–5)

A very similar idea comes in Psalm 24, where the author also asks: "Who shall ascend the hill of the LORD? / And who shall stand in his holy place?" (v. 3). Once again, the concept of "holy mountain" is associated with God's presence in the sanctuary. As in Psalm 15, those who are permitted to ascend the mountain must display characteristics compatible with holiness: "He who has clean hands and a pure heart, / who does not lift up his soul to what is false / and does not swear deceitfully" (Ps. 24:4). Although brief, the answer recalls the obligations of the Sinai covenant, especially the instructions in Leviticus regarding purity. The mention of "clean hands" and "pure heart" highlights the importance of moral holiness. This is the hallmark of those who will inhabit God's holy city.

Conclusion

The concept of God living on a holy mountain is a significant theme in the Old Testament. However, this same theme frames the entire Bible. It begins with the garden of Eden in Genesis and ends with New Jerusalem in Revelation. In Genesis the elevated location of the garden of Eden is indicated by the fact that a single river flows out of Eden, before dividing to become four rivers. Genesis 2:10–14 provides a short and enigmatic description of these rivers. While there is some uncertainty about the identity of all four rivers, the description implies that the garden of Eden occupies a raised position in the middle of the world. In keeping with this picture, the prophet Ezekiel designates Eden as both "the garden of God" and "the holy mountain of God" (Ezek. 28:13–16).

Leaping to the New Testament, the concept of a holy mountain city is linked to New Jerusalem. The author of Hebrews passionately exhorts his readers to remain faithful to the new covenant inaugurated by Jesus Christ, rather than returning to the older covenant associated with Mount Sinai. In doing so he makes a brief but noteworthy comment: "But you have come to Mount Zion and to the city of the living God, the heavenly Jerusalem" (Heb. 12:22). A similar picture is found in the book of Revelation. In chapter 21 the apostle

John records that an angel carried him away "in the Spirit to a great, high mountain" and showed him "the holy city Jerusalem coming down out of heaven from God" (v. 10). In both contexts, the mountain location of New Jerusalem resonates with the pattern found in the Old Testament. God dwells in a holy mountain city, and those who will dwell with him must be holy in order to live within this exalted metropolis.

Viewed in its broader literary context, the whole exodus-Sinai story looks forward to the restoration of the harmonious situation that existed between God and humanity prior to Adam and Eve's rebellion against God in the garden of Eden. With its emphasis upon the need to be made holy in order to ascend into God's presence, the exodus-Sinai story provides a model of how salvation will come through the death of Jesus Christ, the ultimate Passover sacrifice. Citizenship in God's holy city belongs only to those who are sanctified by God.

4

The Royal City

Within the Old Testament, the city of Jerusalem is depicted in a rich variety of ways. As we have observed in the preceding two chapters, Jerusalem is portrayed as a temple-city and a holy mountain. To these significant characteristics may be added the idea of Jerusalem as a royal city. God reigns from Jerusalem as King of kings, as Mount Zion becomes the location of his earthly temple or palace, modeled on his heavenly abode.

This royal dimension stands alongside the concept of holy mountain in Exodus 15. In looking to the future, the redeemed Israelites announce in song: "You will bring them in and plant them on your own mountain, / the place, O Lord, which you have made for your abode, / the sanctuary, O Lord, which your hands have established" (Ex. 15:17). Immediately after this they proclaim, "The Lord will reign forever and ever" (v. 18). God's sovereignty is closely associated with his mountain sanctuary.

God Reigns in Zion

Of the many passages that speak of God as king, Psalm 99 provides one of the most striking descriptions of God reigning from Mount Zion, his holy mountain abode:[1]

The LORD reigns; let the peoples tremble!
>   He sits enthroned upon the cherubim; let the earth quake!
The LORD is great in Zion;
>   he is exalted over all the peoples.
Let them praise your great and awesome name!
>   Holy is he!
The King in his might loves justice.
>   You have established equity;
you have executed justice
>   and righteousness in Jacob.
Exalt the LORD our God;
>   worship at his footstool!
>   Holy is he!

Moses and Aaron were among his priests,
>   Samuel also was among those who called upon his
>   name.
They called to the LORD, and he answered them.
In the pillar of the cloud he spoke to them;
>   they kept his testimonies
>   and the statute that he gave them.

O LORD our God, you answered them;
>   you were a forgiving God to them,
>   but an avenger of their wrongdoings.

---

1. A number of the psalms immediately preceding Psalm 99 also focus on the kingship of God. See Pss. 93:1; 96:10; 97:1.

Exalt the LORD our God,
> and worship at his holy mountain;
> for the LORD our God is holy! (Ps. 99:1–9)

The author of Psalm 99 conveys well the sense of the Lord's holy majesty, climaxing his call to worship with a reference to God's "holy mountain."

The theme of God reigning is also prominent in Psalm 47, which speaks of God having gone up (v. 5) and sitting on his holy throne (v. 8). While there is no explicit mention of Mount Zion in this psalm, it is immediately followed by Psalm 48, in which Mount Zion is extolled as "the city of the great King" (v. 2). A similar picture of the Lord as king on his holy mountain comes in Psalm 24, where the "King of glory" passes through the "ancient doors" to enter his holy dwelling place. Psalm 76 also highlights at length God's majesty by recalling how he has established Jerusalem as his earthly abode.

These references by no means exhaust what is said in the Psalter regarding the Lord reigning on Mount Zion. They are the tip of the iceberg. As Ollenburger observes, "Among the variety of ways in which Yahweh is represented as present upon Mount Zion the most prominent is as king."[2]

Jerusalem is most obviously a royal city because the sovereign Lord of heaven and earth dwells there. However, Jerusalem is also a royal city due to the fact that it is the capital of a kingdom over which a unique human dynasty rules. A strong bond is forged in the Old Testament between the divine king and the earthly king, underscoring the significance of Jerusalem as a royal city. As we shall see, the establishment of Jerusalem as the city of God is linked to the Davidic dynasty, anticipating how Jesus Christ, as Messiah, will establish the ultimate city of God.

---

2. B. C. Ollenburger, *Zion, City of the Great King: A Theological Symbol of the Jerusalem Cult*, JSOTSup 41 (Sheffield, UK: JSOT Press, 1987), 23.

God's Vice-Regent Rules from Jerusalem

The link between Mount Zion as God's sanctuary and the Davidic dynasty is emphasized in Psalm 78 where God's choice of David as ruler over Israel is intimately bound to his choice of Mount Zion. The concluding section of the psalm underscores this close connection:

> He [God] rejected the tent of Joseph;
>> he did not choose the tribe of Ephraim,
> but he chose the tribe of Judah,
>> Mount Zion, which he loves.
> He built his sanctuary like the high heavens,
>> like the earth, which he has founded forever.
> He chose David his servant
>> and took him from the sheepfolds;
> from following the nursing ewes he brought him
>> to shepherd Jacob his people,
>> Israel his inheritance.
> With upright heart he shepherded them
>> and guided them with his skillful hand. (Ps. 78:67–72)

The content of these verses refers to the time of the prophet Samuel and alludes briefly to the narrative recorded in 1 Samuel 3 through 2 Samuel 7.

The emphasis given in the final part of Psalm 78 to God's choosing both Zion and David is linked in a noteworthy way to God's rejection of the tribe of Ephraim and Shiloh as the location for his tent (Ps. 78:60).[3] The juxtaposition of God's rejecting Ephraim and Shiloh and choosing David and Mount Zion is part of a major theme that finds its roots in the book of Genesis. While it is often assumed that

---

3. Shiloh lies in the tribal region of Ephraim.

the origins of Israel's monarchy are to be traced back merely to the time of Samuel, the biblical tradition presents the Davidic monarchy as having a long and noteworthy prehistory.

The expectation of a future Israelite monarchy is introduced within the Abraham narrative of Genesis. In the context of the covenant of circumcision, God promises Abraham and Sarah that kings will be among their descendants (Gen. 17:6, 16). This promise is associated with Abraham's son Isaac, for the eternal covenant established between God and Abraham is closely linked to the unique lineage that descends from Abraham.[4] Moreover, as Abraham himself is to be the spiritual father of many nations, bringing God's blessing to them, the fulfillment of this promise is subsequently linked to a future royal descendant. Within the Abraham narrative itself, this expectation emerges in the oath that God makes to Abraham after the latter demonstrates his willingness to sacrifice, on God's instruction, his much-loved son Isaac. After the angel of the Lord intervenes to save Isaac, God swears a remarkable oath to Abraham. The first part of the divine oath in Genesis 22:16–18 emphasizes Abraham's numerous offspring, but God's concluding words draw attention to a future individual through whom the nations of the earth will be blessed.[5]

In due course the promise of a royal descendant is reflected in the paternal blessing given by Isaac to Jacob in Genesis 27. Mistakenly assuming that he is blessing his firstborn son, Esau, Isaac pronounces an extraordinary blessing upon Jacob:

> See, the smell of my son
>> is as the smell of a field that the Lord has blessed!

---

4. Gen. 17:19–21 emphasizes that the covenant will be established with Isaac and not Ishmael, even though the latter is circumcised, as are other male members of Abraham's household.

5. T. Desmond Alexander, "Further Observations of the Term 'Seed' in Genesis," *TynBul* 48 (1997): 363–67.

> May God give you of the dew of heaven
>> and of the fatness of the earth
>> and plenty of grain and wine.
> Let peoples serve you,
>> and nations bow down to you.
> Be lord over your brothers,
>> and may your mother's sons bow down to you.
> Cursed be everyone who curses you,
>> and blessed be everyone who blesses you!
>>> (Gen. 27:27–29)

The expectation inherent in this blessing is extraordinary, given that the patriarchs are merely recently arrived seminomadic dwellers in the land of Canaan. Isaac speaks of peoples serving and nations bowing down to his son. Moreover, Isaac's concluding remarks about cursing and blessing create a direct link back to the programmatic statement made by God when he invited Abraham to be a blessing to all the families of the earth (Gen. 12:3).

The theme of royalty dominates the opening section of the Joseph story.[6] Various factors support the idea that Jacob views Joseph as a young prince.[7] Privileged by his father and treated as his firstborn son, Joseph wears a distinctive robe, the Hebrew term for which possibly conveys royal connotations.[8] When Joseph has dreams that predict his regal status, his older brothers are deeply offended by these royal expectations. When his brothers subsequently conspire against Joseph and sell him into slavery in Egypt (Gen. 37:12–36), little did they expect that one day they would bow before him, as prime minister of Egypt (Gen. 42:6).

---

6. The expectation of kings ruling in Israel is alluded to in Gen. 36:31: "These are the kings who reigned in the land of Edom, before any king reigned over the Israelites."

7. T. Desmond Alexander, "The Regal Dimension of the תלדות־יעקב: Recovering the Literary Context of Genesis 37–50," in *Reading the Law: Studies in Honour of Gordon J. Wenham*, ed. J. G. McConville and K. Möller, LHBOTS (Edinburgh: T&T Clark, 2007), 196–212.

8. Joseph's firstborn status is noted in 1 Chron. 5:1–2.

The potential royal line traced from Abraham to Joseph, via Isaac and Jacob, is subsequently linked to Joseph's younger son, Ephraim. When Jacob is near to death, Joseph brings his two sons in order that Jacob might bless them. Joseph comes expecting that his eldest son, Manasseh, will receive the blessing of the firstborn. Very deliberately, however, Jacob crosses over his hands on the heads of the two boys and pronounces the firstborn blessing on Ephraim, the younger of the two boys (Gen. 48:14–20). This establishes the expectation that a future king to lead Israel and bring God's blessing to the nations of the earth will come from the tribe of Ephraim.

Although the author of Genesis is careful to acknowledge the prominence given to Joseph and Ephraim, we should not overlook the significance of the events associated with Judah in Genesis 38. In a book that is especially interested in tracing the lineage of the future royal descendants of Abraham, it should not go unnoticed that Genesis 38 begins by focusing on the offspring of Judah. The chapter records Onan's mistreatment of his sister-in-law, Tamar, following the death of his brother Er. When Onan deliberately refuses to provide offspring for his older brother, he too dies. After this Judah intervenes to prevent a similar misfortune befalling his thirdborn son Shelah; he sends Tamar back to her own family as a childless widow. Some years later Tamar is forced to adopt an exceptionally unusual method of raising up offspring for Er. Through deceit, she has intercourse with the recently widowed Judah. When Tamar becomes pregnant, Judah is oblivious to the fact that he is the child's father. His outrage and hostility toward Tamar is reversed only when she discloses to him that he is the father of her child.

Adding to the significance of this bizarre episode, Tamar gives birth to twin boys. The midwife, anxious to ensure at the birthing that she can identify clearly the firstborn child, ties a scarlet thread around the wrist of the baby being born. Unexpectedly, however, the other twin pushes aside the firstborn and emerges before his twin brother. Consequently, this baby boy is appropriately named Perez, meaning "he who breaks through." Given the frequency in Genesis of younger siblings replacing firstborn brothers,[9] the birth of Perez takes on added significance. While the author of Genesis says little more about Perez, he is identified in a short genealogy at the end of the book of Ruth as the ancestor of the lineage that leads to King David (Ruth 4:18–22).

The unexpected introduction of Perez in Genesis 38, interrupting the Joseph story, helps explain a remarkable transformation that takes place in the character of Judah. In Genesis 37 Judah persuades his brothers to sell Joseph into slavery in Egypt for financial gain, rather than simply have him die of hunger in a pit. Years later, Judah willingly offers himself into slavery in Egypt in order that Joseph's younger brother, Benjamin, might be set free. Judah's self-sacrificing offer stands in stark contrast to his earlier callous selfishness. His experience with Tamar accounts for his change of heart.

While Genesis 48 gives priority to how Jacob blesses Joseph's sons, this is immediately followed by Jacob blessing his own sons. In his deathbed pronouncements concerning his own children, Jacob gives preeminence to both Judah and Joseph. Compared to their siblings, Judah and Joseph receive the fullest and most positive blessings from their dying father. In particular, the blessing given to Judah echoes ideas associated with kingship. Jacob states:

> Judah, your brothers shall praise you;
>> your hand shall be on the neck of your enemies;
>> your father's sons shall bow down before you.
> Judah is a lion's cub;
>> from the prey, my son, you have gone up.

---

9. We see this with Ishmael and Isaac, Esau and Jacob, Reuben and Joseph, Zerah and Perez, Manasseh and Ephraim.

He stooped down; he crouched as a lion
>and as a lioness; who dares rouse him?
The scepter shall not depart from Judah,
>nor the ruler's staff from between his feet,
until tribute comes to him;
>and to him shall be the obedience of the peoples.
Binding his foal to the vine
>and his donkey's colt to the choice vine,
he has washed his garments in wine
>and his vesture in the blood of grapes.
His eyes are darker than wine,
>and his teeth whiter than milk. (Gen. 49:8–12)

The poetic nature of what Jacob says has resulted in various interpretations, especially of verse 10, but the underlying tone implies that kingship will ultimately come from the tribe of Judah.

Beyond the book of Genesis, the tribes of Ephraim and Judah receive special attention. Even before the tribes arrive in Canaan, Joshua (an Ephraimite) and Caleb (a Judahite) speak positively about entering the land of Canaan, in contrast to the negative reports of other spies (Num. 13:1–14:38). In the books of Joshua and Judges, the leadership of the nation is initially with Ephraim, although there are indications that the tribe of Judah has been more effective in taking possession of territory.[10] The tribe of Ephraim is portrayed as gradually becoming corrupt morally, leading to its replacement by the tribe of Judah.[11]

The book of Ruth contributes to this expectation by providing a positive account of the Judahite Boaz, which contrasts sharply with the adverse picture of different Ephraimites in the epilogue to Judges.[12]

---

10. The very detailed list of territory allocated to the tribe of Judah in Josh. 15:1–63 comes before a much less detailed list for Ephraim-Manasseh in Josh. 16:1–17:18.

11. As summarized in Ps. 78:56–72.

12. Eugene H. Merrill, "The Book of Ruth: Narration and Shared Themes," *BSac* 142 (1986): 130–39.

Highlighting Boaz's willingness to be a kinsman-redeemer for Naomi and Ruth, the book of Ruth concludes by describing the birth of their son, Obed, who is also designated a kinsman-redeemer (Ruth 4:14–15). The concluding genealogy traces the ancestry of Boaz back to Perez, but also forward to David (Ruth 4:18–22). All of this adds to the idea that the line of Perez is significant for understanding the importance of the Davidic dynasty.

The close association between Jerusalem and the Davidic dynasty is reflected in the events narrated in 2 Samuel 5–7. After eventually being recognized as king of all Israel, David proceeds to capture the Jebusite city of Jerusalem, establishing it as his capital. Second Samuel 5 describes how David conquers the fortress of Zion and takes up residence there, calling it the "city of David." David's success is attributed to the Lord, for the author of 2 Samuel 5 observes that "David became greater and greater, for the LORD, the God of hosts, was with him" (2 Sam. 5:10).

David's capture of Jerusalem completes the protracted process by which the Israelites take full control of all the land promised to the patriarchs. According to Joshua 15:63, the tribe of Judah had previously failed to seize Jerusalem from the Jebusites. As Groves notes:

> In the biblical narrative Zion was the final Canaanite holdout in the promised land. With its fall, the conquest of Canaan begun by Joshua was completed. Having chosen David to act on his behalf, Yahweh took Zion and completed the conquest. In the same stroke, David and Zion were bound inextricably together.[13]

With the capture of Jerusalem, God's promise to the patriarchs concerning their descendants occupying the land of Canaan is fulfilled.

Having established himself as king over Israel in Jerusalem, David

---

13. J. Alan Groves, "Zion Traditions," in *Dictionary of the Old Testament: Historical Books*, ed. B. T. Arnold and H. G. M. Williamson (Downers Grove, IL: InterVarsity Press, 2005), 1023.

proceeds to bring to Jerusalem the ark of God, the footstool of the Lord of hosts, "who sits enthroned on the cherubim" (2 Sam. 6:2). Although the ark's journey to Jerusalem is interrupted for three months, due to the tragic death of Uzzah, David finally transports the ark into the city with great celebration. This event confirmed God's choice of David as king over Israel. Later, Solomon recalled this at the dedication of the temple.

> Blessed be the LORD, the God of Israel, who with his hand has fulfilled what he promised with his mouth to David my father, saying, "Since the day that I brought my people out of the land of Egypt, I chose no city out of all the tribes of Israel in which to build a house, that my name might be there, and I chose no man as prince over my people Israel; but I have chosen Jerusalem that my name may be there, and I have chosen David to be over my people Israel." (2 Chron. 6:4–6)[14]

Solomon's final comments about God's choosing both Jerusalem and David parallel what is said in Psalm 78:68–72. David and Mount Zion are intimately connected in God's purposes. In God's plan, the establishment of the ultimate holy city will involve the Davidic dynasty.

The Building of Two "Houses"

The ark of the Lord of hosts is initially housed in a tent set up by David. The earthly king, however, is troubled by the fact that he lives in a "house of cedar," while "the ark of God dwells in a tent" (2 Sam. 7:2). David then tells the prophet Nathan of his desire to build a permanent house for God. This will consolidate Jerusalem's claim to be the city of God, the location of his earthly residence.

---

14. Cf. 1 Kings 8:16. It appears likely that the text of 1 Kings is shorter due to homoeoteleuton; 2 Chron. 6:5–6 preserves the more original reading.

Although the prophet Nathan initially responds positively to David's proposal, he subsequently receives from God an oracle for David, challenging David's decision to build a temple/palace.

> But that same night the word of the LORD came to Nathan, "Go and tell my servant David, 'Thus says the LORD: Would you build me a house to dwell in? I have not lived in a house since the day I brought up the people of Israel from Egypt to this day, but I have been moving about in a tent for my dwelling. In all places where I have moved with all the people of Israel, did I speak a word with any of the judges of Israel, whom I commanded to shepherd my people Israel, saying, "Why have you not built me a house of cedar?"'" (2 Sam. 7:4–7)

Reminding David that prior to this time, no one was ever instructed by God to build for him a house of cedar, God's remarks are open to different interpretations. On the one hand, his words may be understood as a rejection of a permanent abode. Understood in this way, God expresses a desire to be able to move from place to place, as he has done previously. On the other hand, God may be implying that David is misguided in assuming that he has the authority to decide where and when God's temple will be constructed.[15]

This latter interpretation seems preferable for at least two reasons. First, in God's message to David, God emphasizes his own role in establishing David as ruler over the Israelites, by defeating David's enemies and making his name great. Having done this, God himself will appoint the place where he will dwell with his people (2 Sam. 7:10). This underlines that God alone will choose the location of his

---

15. See L. K. Fuller Dow, *Images of Zion: Biblical Antecedents for the New Jerusalem*, New Testament Monographs 26 (Sheffield, UK: Sheffield Phoenix Press, 2010), 57–58.

dwelling place. This resembles the emphasis found in Psalm 78 regarding God's choice of both David and Mount Zion (cf. Ps. 132:13). Second, God does not prohibit entirely the erection of a permanent temple in Jerusalem; he merely delays its construction. This suggests that God's explanation in verses 5–7 should not be interpreted as implying divine disapproval of temple building per se.

Although God prohibits David from building a house for him, he announces that he will establish David's house forever. This involves a wordplay on the Hebrew term *bayit*, which has a semantic range that extends the meaning of "house" to cover both a physical building and a household. This latter understanding of *bayit* also emphasizes the concept of dynasty. David will not build a "house" (a physical building) for God, but God will build a "house" (a dynasty) for David. Reassuring David that one of his offspring will succeed him, God promises that David's royal successor, from his own flesh and blood, will build a house for God.

God grants to David and his dynasty a special status. God promises that he will be a father to David's successor and that David's son will be viewed as God's son. In light of this, God promises David: "Your house and your kingdom shall be made sure forever before me. Your throne shall be established forever" (2 Sam. 7:16).

Although David himself is prohibited from building God a palace in Jerusalem, this privilege passed to David's son Solomon.[16] When the temple is finally completed, God's glory fills the new, permanent sanctuary (1 Kings 8:10–11; cf. 2 Chron. 7:1–2). The description of God entering the temple echoes strongly what happens after the portable sanctuary is erected at Mount Sinai (Ex. 40:34–35). The Jerusalem temple supersedes the portable sanctuary, marking the end

---

16. In 1 Chron. 22:8 David tells Solomon that God prevented him from building the temple because he had shed so much blood on the earth. The task of temple building falls to Solomon, whose name implies "peace."

of the Israelites' journey to the Promised Land and confirming the location of God's holy mountain.

Solomon's role in building the Jerusalem temple takes on added significance when we observe how the author of 1 Kings associates Solomon with wisdom. Solomon's wisdom was such that rulers of other nations came to learn from him. His wisdom was literally proverbial, for many of the sayings recorded in the book of Proverbs are attributed to Solomon. Through these wisdom sayings a striking connection is made between God's creation of the world, the construction of the tabernacle and temple, and the making of an Israelite home. Linking these different building activities are the words *wisdom*, *knowledge*, and *understanding*. These three terms are used in combination in Proverbs to describe the divine creation of the cosmos:

> The LORD by wisdom founded the earth;
>> by understanding he established the heavens;
> by his knowledge the deeps broke open,
>> and the clouds drop down the dew. (Prov. 3:19–20)

The same terminology is used to describe how Bezalel and Hiram constructed the portable sanctuary and Jerusalem temple respectively (Ex. 31:3; 35:30–31; 1 Kings 7:13–14). This parallel between the creation of the cosmos and the portable sanctuary/temple is noteworthy because the latter structures were viewed as models of the cosmos. Remarkably, the same qualities required by God to construct the cosmos and by others to manufacture God's earthly residence are also necessary for the making of an Israelite home:

> By wisdom a house is built,
>> and by understanding it is established;
> by knowledge the rooms are filled
>> with all precious and pleasant riches. (Prov. 24:3–4)

These distinctive parallels between the construction of the cosmos, the portable sanctuary/temple, and an ordinary home are in keeping with the idea that God desires to create a temple-city, where he will co-habit with humanity. To participate positively in God's creative activity, people must have wisdom, knowledge, and understanding. Proverbs 2:6 states that these attributes find their origin in God: "For the LORD gives wisdom; / from his mouth come knowledge and understanding."

While the book of Proverbs, associated with Solomon, speaks positively of house building that is undertaken with wisdom from God, the book of Ecclesiastes, written from the perspective of a Davidic king, highlights the futility of building without reference to God. With remarkable candor, the author acknowledges in Ecclesiastes 2:4–11 that no sense of purpose may be found in building enterprises that are undertaken for self-glorification. Although people have a God-given capacity and desire to be constructive, such activity of itself cannot fully satisfy if God is excluded.

Solomon's role in building the temple in Jerusalem reflects the special place of the Davidic dynasty in God's plans for the earth. In light of the divine promises to the patriarchs in Genesis, the expectation exists that a future monarch will rule on God's behalf over the whole earth. This belief permeates Psalm 72, which voices the hope that a Davidic king will one day exercise universal rule. The kingdom associated with this anticipated monarch will be characterized by compassion for the poor and the oppressed (v. 13), with the king bringing justice to those who have been unfairly exploited and harshly treated (vv. 2, 4, 12–14). The psalmist also speaks of the king's rule impacting the mountains and hills, leading to prosperity, righteousness, and fruitfulness (vv. 3, 16). Verse 17 also recalls God's oath to Abraham in Genesis 22:18 regarding the blessing of the nations.[17] By stating that kings will bow

---

17. See Alexander, "Further Observations of the Term "Seed" in Genesis," 363–67.

before this Davidic king and nations will serve him, the psalm echoes the promises given by God to the patriarchs of Genesis.

The association of Mount Zion with the Davidic dynasty provides a second reason for characterizing Jerusalem as a royal city. The Davidic king serves as God's vice-regent. Consequently, two palaces stand adjacent to each other in Jerusalem: the Lord's palace (the temple) and the Davidic palace.

Hostility toward God's Royal City

The concept of Jerusalem as God's royal city is also highlighted through the theme of opposition to the rule of God. Given humanity's hostility toward God, Jerusalem as the city of his presence becomes an object of loathing for those who set themselves against God. The motif of aggressive enemies positioning themselves to overthrow the city and all that it symbolizes is especially evident throughout the Psalter. In response, many psalms recall in vivid imagery the power of God to subdue every enemy that arrogantly stands in opposition to God and his people.

Hostility toward God is prominent within the Psalter. In its final edited form, Psalms 1 and 2 appear to have been deliberately placed at the start of the Psalter as appropriate introductions. If they function as a hermeneutical guide to what follows, then both psalms underscore that humanity is clearly divided between those who side with God and those who oppose him. While the former are promised security and life, the latter are warned that their actions will ultimately result in death. The opening lines of Psalm 2, in particular, highlight the extent of human antagonism toward God:

> Why do the nations rage
>   and the peoples plot in vain?
> The kings of the earth set themselves,

and the rulers take counsel together,

against the LORD and against his anointed, saying,

"Let us burst their bonds apart

and cast away their cords from us." (Ps. 2:1–3)

The psalm then proceeds to focus on how God has responded to this opposition by appointing his king on Zion, his holy hill. The divine declaration that this king is God's son recalls what God says regarding the future Davidic dynasty in 2 Samuel 7:12–16:

When your days are fulfilled and you lie down with your fathers, I will raise up your offspring after you, who shall come from your body, and I will establish his kingdom. He shall build a house for my name, and I will establish the throne of his kingdom forever. I will be to him a father, and he shall be to me a son. (2 Sam. 7:12–14a)

After drawing attention to how God has installed his "son," the king, on Mount Zion, Psalm 2 goes on to challenge the kings and rulers of the earth, inviting them to acknowledge the authority that God has delegated to his "son":

Now therefore, O kings, be wise;

be warned, O rulers of the earth.

Serve the LORD with fear,

and rejoice with trembling.

Kiss the Son,

lest he be angry, and you perish in the way,

for his wrath is quickly kindled.

Blessed are all who take refuge in him. (Ps. 2:10–12)

By giving priority, when compiling the Psalter, to this scene of God responding to human opposition by appointing his king on Zion, the compilers of the Psalter underscore the importance of Jerusalem as a royal city.

Against this setting, running throughout the Psalter are psalms that bring into view, to differing degrees and from different perspectives, the motifs associated with divine power, aggressive enemies, suffering, and victory. Strikingly, Psalm 2 is immediately followed by such a psalm, which, according to its title, focuses ironically on the opposition that King David faces from his own son Absalom. While Psalm 3 reflects the reality of opposition toward God's appointed king, it also looks in confidence to God's deliverance of the righteous from their enemies. Such confidence rests in the knowledge that God has the power to overcome all opponents.

Opposition to God and his anointed one permeates the Psalter. Yet, within its final structure, there is a distinctive movement that affirms God's ultimate victory over all opponents. Whereas Psalm 2 highlights the rebellious spirit of the kings and rulers of the earth as they seek autonomy from God, by the end of the Psalter they are portrayed as being bound and punished as they come under God's judgment.

Praise the LORD!
Sing to the LORD a new song,
     his praise in the assembly of the godly!
Let Israel be glad in his Maker;
     let the children of Zion rejoice in their King!
Let them praise his name with dancing,
     making melody to him with tambourine and lyre!
For the LORD takes pleasure in his people;
     he adorns the humble with salvation.
Let the godly exult in glory;
     let them sing for joy on their beds.

Let the high praises of God be in their throats
    and two-edged swords in their hands,
to execute vengeance on the nations
    and punishments on the peoples,
to bind their kings with chains
    and their nobles with fetters of iron,
to execute on them the judgment written!
    This is honor for all his godly ones.
Praise the LORD! (Ps. 149:1–9)

Conclusion

The establishment of Jerusalem as God's royal city is an important development in the Old Testament story. It marks a partial fulfillment of God's plan to live on the earth in harmony with humans. As the place where God's earthly palace is constructed, Jerusalem takes on special significance. But Jerusalem is also the location from which God's chosen king reigns. At the center of God's earthly kingdom, Mount Zion is set apart as unique. Human resistance to the reign of God on earth also means that Jerusalem becomes the main target of opposition.

Undoubtedly, the belief that God reigned from Jerusalem explains why ancient Israelites viewed the city as preeminent. However, as we shall observe in the next two chapters, the citizens of ancient Jerusalem were largely incapable and unwilling to live lives that reflected a wholehearted, exclusive obedience to God in tune with his holy nature. Their shortcomings, like those of Adam and Eve, would have a profound impact upon the future of the temple-city.

5

Envisaging a Transformed Jerusalem

With the establishment of Jerusalem as God's temple-mountain city during the reigns of David and Solomon, the biblical story reaches an important climax. This marks a significant step toward the fulfillment of God's creation plan. Jerusalem takes on a unique status that distinguishes it from every other earthly city. As reflected in various psalms, the Lord dwells on Mount Zion, having established the Davidic dynasty as the human agency through which God's rule will eventually be extended to cover the whole earth. "Zion represents (at least in its eschatological sense) God's people living in God's place under God's rule."[1]

Although Jerusalem is highly privileged and becomes the center of God's rule on earth, the biblical story records the city's subsequent destruction. As we shall observe in more detail later, the major prophetic books of Isaiah, Jeremiah, and Ezekiel all concentrate on

---

1. H. A. Thomas, "Zion," in *Dictionary of the Old Testament: Prophets*, ed. M. J. Boda and J. G. McConville (Downers Grove, IL: IVP Academic, 2012), 912.

how God abandons Jerusalem, permitting the Babylonians to raze its walls and demolish the temple. With the fall of Jerusalem in 586 BC the Davidic dynasty loses control of the city and the surrounding region. Everything that the Lord enabled David and Solomon to achieve in establishing Jerusalem as the holy city of God is dramatically undone.

To explain why this occurred, the book of Kings recounts a selected history of the events leading up to the Babylonian overthrow of Jerusalem. Even the reign of Solomon is a harbinger of what lies ahead. Disregarding the instructions provided in the Law of Moses (Deut. 17:16–17), Solomon amasses great wealth, imports horses from Egypt, and marries foreign wives, who promote idolatry within Jerusalem (1 Kings 10:14–11:8). Solomon's extensive kingdom is subsequently divided. His son Rehoboam continues to exercise authority in Jerusalem, but only because of God's commitment to David (1 Kings 11:36). The book of Kings records the checkered history of the Davidic dynasty, highlighting how the failure of the monarchy contributes significantly to the punishment of Jerusalem. As the author of Kings underlines, the destruction of Jerusalem and the exiling of its population are directly related to the population's failure to remain loyal and obedient to the Lord. Although the Israelites enjoyed the privilege of dwelling with God on his holy mountain, they forfeited this by failing to keep their covenant obligation.

At Mount Sinai, God set out the requirements for holy living for those who would later dwell on his holy mountain. Unfortunately, by their unrighteous behavior the Israelite inhabitants of Jerusalem repeatedly desecrated God's holy dwelling place. The author of Chronicles, in his short description of Zedekiah's reign, conveys well the rebellious nature of the people:

Zedekiah was twenty-one years old when he began to reign, and he reigned eleven years in Jerusalem. He did what was evil in the sight of the LORD his God. He did not humble himself before Jeremiah the prophet, who spoke from the mouth of the LORD. He also rebelled against King Nebuchadnezzar, who had made him swear by God. He stiffened his neck and hardened his heart against turning to the LORD, the God of Israel. All the officers of the priests and the people likewise were exceedingly unfaithful, following all the abominations of the nations. And they polluted the house of the LORD that he had made holy in Jerusalem. (2 Chron. 36:11–14)

In light of how the people of Jerusalem abused their privileged position, it is no surprise that they were frequently denounciated sternly by God through his prophets.[2]

God's Condemnation of Jerusalem's Citizens through Isaiah

The prophet Isaiah vividly conveys God's condemnation of those living in Jerusalem during the eighth century BC. As Peterson ably observes:

For Isaiah, words are watercolors and melodies and chisels to make truth and beauty and goodness. Or, as the case may be, hammers and swords and scalpels to unmake sin and guilt and rebellion. Isaiah does not merely convey information. He creates visions, delivers revelation, arouses belief. He is a poet in the most fundamental sense—a *maker*, making God present and that presence urgent. Isaiah is the supreme poet-prophet to come out of the Hebrew people.[3]

---

2. For a survey of prophetic denouncements of Jerusalem, see F. Poulsen, *Representing Zion: Judgement and Salvation in the Old Testament*, Copenhagen International Seminar (New York: Routledge, 2015).

3. Eugene H. Peterson, "Isaiah: Introduction," in *The Message: The Bible in Contemporary Language: Numbered Edition* (Colorado Springs: NavPress, 2005), 912; emphasis original.

The opening words of the book of Isaiah are a damning indictment of Jerusalem's population, emphasizing their failure to acknowledge the Lord as their sovereign master:

> Hear, O heavens, and give ear, O earth;
>   for the LORD has spoken:
> "Children have I reared and brought up,
>   but they have rebelled against me.
> The ox knows its owner,
>   and the donkey its master's crib,
> but Israel does not know,
>   my people do not understand."
>
> Ah, sinful nation,
>   a people laden with iniquity,
> offspring of evildoers,
>   children who deal corruptly!
> They have forsaken the LORD,
>   they have despised the Holy One of Israel,
>   they are utterly estranged. (Isa. 1:2–4)

This stinging criticism of Jerusalem underscores the failure of the people to be righteous. By forsaking the Lord, they were no better than the ancient inhabitants of Sodom and Gomorrah (Isa. 1:10). So sinful and misguided were the rulers of Jerusalem that even their sacrifices and religious practices were abhorrent to God (Isa. 1:11–15). Ironically, the very sacrifices that were meant to atone for the people's sins offended God. Underlying God's antipathy toward the people of Jerusalem, especially their leaders, was their moral failure to ensure justice for the socially marginalized.

> How the faithful city
>   has become a whore,
>   she who was full of justice!

Righteousness lodged in her,
>   but now murderers.
Your silver has become dross,
>   your best wine mixed with water.
Your princes are rebels
>   and companions of thieves.
Everyone loves a bribe
>   and runs after gifts.
They do not bring justice to the fatherless,
>   and the widow's cause does not come to them.
>   (Isa. 1:21–23)

Against this background, the Lord's message communicated through Isaiah called for a change of heart and behavior:

Wash yourselves; make yourselves clean;
>   remove the evil of your deeds from before my eyes;
cease to do evil,
>   learn to do good;
seek justice,
>   correct oppression;
bring justice to the fatherless,
>   plead the widow's cause. (Isa. 1:16–17)

The indictment leveled against the rulers of Jerusalem, and even the call to repent, paints a disturbing picture of a morally corrupt city. The mountain of God is anything but holy. The book of Isaiah repeatedly returns to highlighting the discrepancy between what Jerusalem ought to be as God's city and how it was in reality in Isaiah's time.[4]

---

4. For a broader discussion of how other prophets echoed Isaiah's condemnation of those with economic and political power in Jerusalem, see Leslie J. Hoppe, *The Holy City: Jerusalem in the Theology of the Old Testament* (Collegeville, MN: Liturgical Press, 2000), 73–98.

Isaiah Anticipates the Fall of Jerusalem

In light of the city's corruption, Isaiah warned of coming judgment, with God's wrath being directed against the city's inhabitants. Reflecting this outcome, the present book of Isaiah can be divided into two distinct halves: chapters 1–39 and 40–66. Whereas chapters 1–39 are set against historical events associated with the eighth century BC Judean kings, Uzziah (767/766–736/735; coregent from 785; not active after 750 BC); J(eh)otham (752/751–732/731 BC); Ahaz (732/731–716 BC; coregent from 736/35 BC); and Hezekiah (716–687/686 BC; coregent from 729 BC), chapters 40–66 reflect events that will take place after the sacking of Jerusalem by the Babylonians in 586 BC. In its final form, the contents of the book of Isaiah describe events that not only span several centuries but also look forward to the eschaton.[5]

The destruction of Jerusalem is recorded briefly in 2 Kings 25. Given God's desire to create a holy city as his dwelling place on earth, the decimation of Jerusalem by the Babylonians is highly ironic. As we have already observed, Genesis 11:1–9 describes how Babel/Babylon was founded as the antithesis to the city of God. With the Babylonian invasion of Jerusalem in 586 BC, all that God had patiently done to establish his temple-city was reduced to ashes and

---

5. Scholars differ on how the book of Isaiah should be understood, with many in the last two centuries being persuaded that its contents come largely from three different authors. In broad terms, Proto-Isaiah produced chaps. 1–39, Deutero-Isaiah produced chaps. 40–55, and Trito-Isaiah produced chaps. 56–66. The basic reasoning for this analysis rests on the fact that chaps. 1–39 reflect a setting in the late eighth century, chaps. 40–55 appear to address the late sixth century, and chaps. 56–66 come from an even later stage when disillusionment about the restoration of Jerusalem after the Babylonian exile prompted a late postexilic writer to imagine and promote astonishingly positive expectations about the future of Jerusalem. For a short summary of this approach, see John Goldingay, *The Theology of the Book of Isaiah* (Downers Grove, IL: InterVarsity Press, 2014), 12–13. An alternative analysis of Isaiah would suggest that an eighth-century Isaiah was responsible for the whole book, with chaps. 40–48 predicting a return to Jerusalem after the Babylonian exile, and chaps. 49–66 looking even further into the future, anticipating a time when God's deliverance of the earth from the powers of evil would be fully achieved. Significantly, no mention is made of Babylon after chap. 48 (see C. T. Begg, "Babylon in the Book of Isaiah," in *The Book of Isaiah*, ed. J. Vermeylen [Leuven: Leuven University Press, 1989], 121–25). This latter approach is the one favored here.

rubble. Babylon appeared victorious. Yet this was not the end of the story, for Isaiah speaks words of comfort, promising restoration and the creation of a radically different Jerusalem.

By predicting a Babylonian victory, the prophet Isaiah appeared to contradict all that Jerusalem/Mount Zion stood for. Moreover, this surprising outcome seems to set in reverse God's plan to inhabit the earth. Not surprisingly, therefore, the idea of Jerusalem falling to the Babylonians presented a major theological dilemma for the people of Jerusalem and Judah. Nations being hostile toward Jerusalem, the holy mountain of God, was accepted as an inevitable consequence of humanity's opposition to the rule of God on earth, but the people of Jerusalem believed that God's presence and that of the Davidic kings ensured the city's invincibility. God's enemies would be overthrown and his rule extended throughout the earth.

While the prophet Isaiah clearly anticipates the Babylonian overthrow of Jerusalem, he deliberately structures his book carefully to show that the downfall of Jerusalem is not a consequence simply of internal political weakness in the face of external military power. Isaiah emphasizes that the fall of Jerusalem is unquestioningly due to divine judgment, with God using the Babylonians as agents of punishment. To draw this out, the first half of Isaiah brings into view the activity of others who sought unsuccessfully to overthrow Jerusalem. Their failure underscored that God had the power to deliver Jerusalem if he so chose.

Isaiah 7 begins by noting how Jerusalem is protected by God when threatened by a coalition involving Aram and the northern kingdom of Israel: "In the days of Ahaz the son of Jotham, son of Uzziah, king of Judah, Rezin the king of Syria and Pekah the son of Remaliah the king of Israel came up to Jerusalem to wage war against it, but could not yet mount an attack against it" (Isa. 7:1). While this opening verse reassuringly indicates that Jerusalem will be secure from the threat posed by a Syro-Ephraimite alliance, much of the material in Isaiah 7–11 is highly critical of King Ahaz and his failure as a Davidic king to trust the Lord. Yet, in spite of this criticism of Ahaz, chapter 12 offers a very positive statement of what God will do in the future for Jerusalem:

You will say in that day:

> "I will give thanks to you, O Lord,
>> for though you were angry with me,
> your anger turned away,
>> that you might comfort me.

> "Behold, God is my salvation;
>> I will trust, and will not be afraid;
> for the Lord God is my strength and my song,
>> and he has become my salvation."

With joy you will draw water from the wells of salvation. And you will say in that day:

> "Give thanks to the Lord,
>> call upon his name,
> make known his deeds among the peoples,
>> proclaim that his name is exalted.

> "Sing praises to the Lord, for he has done gloriously;
>> let this be made known in all the earth.
> Shout, and sing for joy, O inhabitant of Zion,
>> for great in your midst is the Holy One of Israel."
>>> (Isa. 12:1–6)

Chapters 13–23 consist mainly of oracles against the nations, but even here occasional glimpses of hope are given, reflecting God's ongoing commitment to Jerusalem. Isaiah 14:32 affirms, "The Lord has founded Zion, / and in her the afflicted of his people find refuge." Similarly, Isaiah 18:7 records: "At that time tribute will be brought to the Lord of hosts / from a people tall and smooth, / from a people feared near and far, / a nation mighty and conquering, / whose land the rivers divide, / to Mount Zion, the place of the name of the Lord of hosts." A further statement of God's commitment to Zion comes in Isaiah 24:23: "Then the moon will be confounded / and the sun ashamed, / for the Lord of hosts reigns / on Mount Zion and in Jerusalem, / and his glory will be before his elders." To these, Isaiah 28:16–17 adds the expectation of God's building up Zion through a future "cornerstone," a metaphor for a promised king. God's protection of Zion in the face of foreign foes is mentioned in Isaiah 29:5–8, and the restoration of exiles to Zion is graphically described with vivid images of new life in Isaiah 35:1–10. With "everlasting joy" "the ransomed of the Lord shall return and come to Zion with singing" (Isa. 35:10).

The positive picture of God restoring exiles to Zion in Isaiah 35 is immediately followed by two episodes that focus on the divine rescue of King Hezekiah, first from the Assyrians (chaps. 36–37) and then from illness (chap. 38). God's deliverance of the king and Jerusalem from the Assyrians takes on added significance in the light of how the Assyrians decimated the northern kingdom of Israel in 722 BC.[6]

These expressions of hope scattered throughout the book of Isaiah are exceptionally important. The book of Isaiah radiates a confidence that, in spite of the abject failure of eighth-century Jerusalem to be the city of God, the Lord will accomplish his plan to construct a temple-city on a holy mountain. Yet the expectation of forthcoming divine punishment remains a real threat if the people continue

---

6. Cf. L. K. Fuller Dow, *Images of Zion: Biblical Antecedents for the New Jerusalem*, New Testament Monographs 26 (Sheffield, UK: Sheffield Phoenix Press, 2010), 89.

to desecrate God's dwelling place through idolatry and injustice. Unfortunately, Isaiah's predictions of chastisement become a reality in the sixth century BC.

Isaiah's Visions of a New Jerusalem

Although Isaiah predicts a future time when Jerusalem will be abandoned by God, his prophecies, which span many years, also anticipate a time when the temple-city will be thoroughly renovated. Responding to the tragic picture of an immoral city, the prophet Isaiah predicts the future transformation of Jerusalem into a righteous city that will be the place of salvation for the nations. As Webb notes:

> The vision of the book moves, in fact, from the historical Jerusalem of the eighth century (under judgment) to New Jerusalem of the eschaton, which is the centre of the new cosmos and symbol of the new age. To this new Jerusalem the nations come (66:18–21; cf. 60:1–22) so that ultimately the nations find their salvation in Zion.[7]

The picture of a radically different Jerusalem is conveyed most fully in oracles recorded toward the end of the book. Yet the transformation of Jerusalem is introduced as a significant expectation in the opening chapters. Looking to the future, Isaiah predicts a time when Jerusalem, as "the mountain of the house of the LORD," will become the center of a fundamentally different world (Isa. 2:2–5).

The imagery used in Isaiah 2:2–5 echoes older traditions that may be traced back to Mount Sinai. Isaiah foresees a time when the nations will come to the mountain of God in order to be instructed in the ways of God. Recalling the Israelites' experience at Mount Sinai

---

7. Barry G. Webb, "Zion in Transformation: A Literary Approach to Isaiah," in *The Bible in Three Dimensions*, ed. D. J. A. Clines, S. E. Fowl, and S. E. Porter, JSOTSup 87 (Sheffield, UK: JSOT Press, 1990), 71.

in the past, the word of the Lord shall go forth from Mount Zion. Exalted as king, the Lord shall pass judgment on disputes, bringing universal peace and an end to war.[8]

While Isaiah unambiguously declares that Jerusalem will be punished for her unrighteousness, he also anticipates restoration after judgment. As Thomas remarks:

> Isaiah 25–27 gives a particular vision of this renewal, where death will no longer be operative (Is 25), peace will be the banner of the city (Is 26) and God's vineyard of delight will produce fruit over the face of the world (Is 27). Further, nations will come and worship at the renewed sanctuary in Zion (Is 27:13; cf. Is 2:2–3). Key to Isaiah 25–26 is the vision of the judged yet restored "mountain of God" and "city"—Zion and Jerusalem.[9]

These remarkable expectations regarding a transformed Jerusalem are developed further in the final chapters of the book. In Isaiah 60, the prophet foresees a time when God's presence, typified by light and glory, will fill a renewed Jerusalem, driving out the darkness that covers the world (Isa. 60:2). The imagery of light and darkness, along with glory, recalls the exodus experience.

Concerning God's rejection of Jerusalem, Isaiah proclaims hope by announcing the Lord's intention to transform Jerusalem into the most splendid of cities. Through his active involvement God will secure a glorious future for the city and its inhabitants:

> Whereas you [Jerusalem/Zion] have been forsaken and
>   hated,
>   with no one passing through,

---

8. The Lord's role as judge echoes the experience of the Israelites at Mount Sinai, as reflected in Ex. 18:13–26 and the prominence given to the judgments within the book of the covenant (Ex. 21:1–22:20).

9. Thomas, "Zion," 911.

I will make you majestic forever,
    a joy from age to age.
You shall suck the milk of nations;
    you shall nurse at the breast of kings;
and you shall know that I, the LORD, am your Savior
    and your Redeemer, the Mighty One of Jacob.

Instead of bronze I will bring gold,
    and instead of iron I will bring silver;
instead of wood, bronze,
    instead of stones, iron.
I will make your overseers peace
    and your taskmasters righteousness.
Violence shall no more be heard in your land,
    devastation or destruction within your borders;
you shall call your walls Salvation,
    and your gates Praise. (Isa. 60:15–18)

As God's presence brings light to the entire city (Isa. 60:19–20), this transformed Jerusalem/Zion will be characterized by joy, peace, and righteousness. This positive picture of a new Jerusalem is developed further in Isaiah 62:1–5. The corruption and immorality of Jerusalem's past is irreversibly replaced by a righteousness that shines forth. No longer abandoned by God, Jerusalem will become a precious jewel in the Lord's hand, a witness to the nations that this is indeed the city of God.

In describing the transformation of Jerusalem, the book of Isaiah introduces the idea that this new Jerusalem is not a city created through a slow process of evolution. On the contrary, Isaiah emphasizes that this ideal city owes its very existence to the creative activity of God. Using language that echoes the opening chapter of Genesis, Isaiah quotes God as saying:

For behold, I create new heavens
   and a new earth,
and the former things shall not be remembered
   or come into mind.
But be glad and rejoice forever
   in that which I create;
for behold, I create Jerusalem to be a joy,
   and her people to be a gladness. (Isa. 65:17–18)

Recalling the Genesis 1 portrayal of creation, the Lord speaks here of creating "new heavens and a new earth" (v. 17). Remarkably, this announcement is followed almost immediately by a parallel statement that God will "create Jerusalem" (v. 18). In both instances, God uses the same Hebrew verb—*bara'*, "to create"—implying that Jerusalem is to be equated with the new heavens and a new earth. This resonates with the larger biblical picture, for God's purpose in creating the earth is to dwell in a temple-city that will fill the whole world. To underline the radical transformation that will accompany God's creation of the cosmic new Jerusalem, the oracle goes on to speak of how human life will be changed (Isa. 65:19–24). And after emphasizing how the city's human inhabitants will enjoy peace and security, God describes how this transformation will impact the animals living on his holy mountain: "'The wolf and the lamb shall graze together; / the lion shall eat straw like the ox, / and dust shall be the serpent's food. / They shall not hurt or destroy / in all my holy mountain,' / says the LORD" (Isa. 65:25).[10]

Looking to the future transformation of Jerusalem, Isaiah brings together in close association the concepts of holy mountain,

---

10. Gordon McConville, "Jerusalem in the Old Testament," in *Jerusalem Past and Present in the Purposes of God*, ed. P. W. L. Walker (Croydon, UK: Deo Gloria Trust, 1992), 36, writes, "By the end of Isaiah, Zion is understood as God's glorified people in a new creation which is at the end of time and on a cosmic scale."

Jerusalem, and new heavens and a new earth (cf. Isa. 66:18–23). We continue to see the significance of the city as the climax to God's awe-inspiring rejuvenation of the earth, the place where he and people will dwell together in harmony.

While the origins of Isaiah's expectations may be traced back to much earlier times, these passages anticipate events still to take place. The hope offered is designed to sustain those who long for the establishment of the city of God in all its glory. The passages from Isaiah quoted above illustrate, but do not exhaust, the prophet's expectations regarding a divinely transformed Jerusalem. Everything points toward the restoration of the comprehensive harmony that existed in the garden of Eden prior to Adam and Eve's rebellion against God. But Eden will no longer be simply a garden; it will become a majestic, cosmopolitan city.[11]

This vision of an eschatological new Jerusalem is not just wishful thinking on the part of Isaiah. He uses this dramatic picture of a transformed city as a reason for the eighth-century inhabitants of Jerusalem to reform their ways and walk in light of the Lord. He passionately summons the people of Jerusalem to return to the Lord and to live righteously as citizens of the holy city.

The Servant King in Isaiah

Throughout the book of Isaiah, expectations regarding the creation of a radically new Jerusalem are intimately connected with the transformation of the Davidic dynasty. The future destiny of Jerusalem

---

11. Throughout Isaiah there are indications that the eschatological city will be populated by people from every nation. E.g., Isa. 19:22–25 states: "The Lord will strike Egypt, striking and healing, and they will return to the Lord, and he will listen to their pleas for mercy and heal them. In that day there will be a highway from Egypt to Assyria, and Assyria will come into Egypt, and Egypt into Assyria, and the Egyptians will worship with the Assyrians. In that day Israel will be the third with Egypt and Assyria, a blessing in the midst of the earth, whom the Lord of hosts has blessed, saying, 'Blessed be Egypt my people, and Assyria the work of my hands, and Israel my inheritance.'"

is tied to the destiny of the monarchy. As Clements observes, two themes "form the backbone of the entire Isaiah book": "God's chosen dynasty of kings and the glory of the holy city from which it ruled."[12]

We have already noted that the book of Isaiah begins by condemning the immorality of the eighth-century citizens of Jerusalem. The divine oracles denouncing Jerusalem are directed especially toward the city's leadership. Despite God's special relationship with the Davidic monarchy, the successive kings reigning in Jerusalem are viewed as being both morally corrupt and lacking faith in the Lord. In light of the failure of his chosen line of vice-regents, the divine king commissions Isaiah to warn the Davidic rulers of Jerusalem. Occurring in the aftermath of the death of King Uzziah, Isaiah's awe-inspiring vision of the holy, divine king enthroned in the sanctuary prepares him well for his encounters with future Davidic kings (Isa. 6:1–13).

Confronting King Ahaz, Isaiah challenges him regarding his failure to trust the Lord when confronted by a Syro-Ephraimite alliance. By looking to Assyria for assistance, rather than to God, Ahaz exacerbates the crisis. Against the background of Ahaz's faithlessness as God's vice-regent, Isaiah 9:1–7 anticipates the coming of a new and better Davidic king:

> For to us a child is born,
>> to us a son is given;
> and the government shall be upon his shoulder,
>> and his name shall be called
> Wonderful Counselor, Mighty God,
>> Everlasting Father, Prince of Peace.
> Of the increase of his government and of peace
>> there will be no end,

12. Ronald E. Clements, "The Davidic Covenant in the Isaiah Tradition," in *Covenant as Context: Essays in Honour of E. W. Nicholson*, ed. A. D. H. Mayes and R. B. Salters (New York: Oxford University Press, 2003), 65.

on the throne of David and over his kingdom,
    to establish it and to uphold it
with justice and with righteousness
    from this time forth and forevermore.
The zeal of the LORD of hosts will do this. (Isa. 9:6–7)

Later in Isaiah, a further oracle is recorded, describing how a shoot will spring up from the stump of Jesse, a metaphor that pictures the renewing of a "chopped-down" Davidic dynasty:

There shall come forth a shoot from the stump of Jesse,
    and a branch from his roots shall bear fruit.
And the Spirit of the LORD shall rest upon him,
    the Spirit of wisdom and understanding,
    the Spirit of counsel and might,
    the Spirit of knowledge and the fear of the LORD.
And his delight shall be in the fear of the LORD.
He shall not judge by what his eyes see,
    or decide disputes by what his ears hear,
but with righteousness he shall judge the poor,
    and decide with equity for the meek of the earth;
and he shall strike the earth with the rod of his mouth,
    and with the breath of his lips he shall kill the
        wicked.
Righteousness shall be the belt of his waist,
    and faithfulness the belt of his loins. (Isa. 11:1–5)

Sharing much in common, these two passages describe a future Davidic king who will govern wisely, bringing justice to the poor and oppressed. Given the absence of righteousness within eighth-century Jerusalem, these predictions of a truly righteous Davidic king herald a new age. By speaking of a "shoot from the stump of Jesse," God signals that the present Davidic dynasty will be ended in order for a new beginning to be made.

An overview of Isaiah 7–11 reveals that God will punish the house of David for its failure to rule appropriately as his vice-regent. Yet God will not abandon completely the Davidic dynasty; he will renew it through raising up a Spirit-filled king who will govern with wisdom and justice and will bring peace to the world. The hopes associated with this future Davidic king resonate strongly with Isaiah's visions of a renewed Jerusalem. This future Davidic king will exercise universal influence, bringing back to Jerusalem those who have been scattered among the nations (Isa. 11:10–12). Moreover, the rule of this righteous king is linked to the transformation of the natural environment (Isa. 11:6–9; cf. 65:25). "The future kingdom is described as something similar to a paradise with peace and security, even the removal of the original curse on the relationship between man and the animals (Gen 3:14–19). Natural enemies in the animal kingdom will live together, feed together, and play together, but the strong or poisonous beasts will not harm anyone."[13]

These oracles of hope in Isaiah 7–12 for the renewing of Zion through a future Davidic king are placed in the reign of Ahaz. Further oracles come in Isaiah 28–39 linked to the reign of Hezekiah, Ahaz's successor. These also present a less than hopeful picture regarding the Davidic dynasty in the eighth century BC, for Hezekiah is warned against the danger of trusting in Egypt when threatened by the Assyrians. Jerusalem, however, is spared from destruction when God intervenes, an event that underlines God's special commitment to both Zion and the Davidic dynasty.

The defeat of the Assyrians is merely a temporary reprieve, however, for Isaiah 39 contains a divine oracle that warns of a future deportation

---

13. Gary V. Smith, *Isaiah 1–39*, NAC 15A (Nashville: B&H, 2007), 273.

of the royal family to Babylonia. The contents of chapter 39 are note-worthy, because they create a remarkable bridge between the first part of Isaiah and chapters 40–48. Chapters 1–39 concentrate mainly on the eighth-century reigns of Ahaz and Hezekiah, but chapters 40–48 look to the future, anticipating how in the late sixth century the Persian ruler Cyrus will overthrow Babylon, making it possible for Judean exiles to return to the decimated city of Jerusalem.

Isaiah 39 describes how Hezekiah, after recovering from a serious illness, receives envoys from the king of Babylon. Hezekiah not only welcomes the Babylonian envoys, but he seizes the opportunity to impress them by showing off all his wealth; everything is shown to them. Apart from possibly wishing to impress his foreign visitors regarding his own status as a great king, Hezekiah may have hoped to forge a political and military alliance with the Babylonians against the powerful Assyrians.

However, Hezekiah's actions anger God. Hezekiah should have known better than to look to Babylon, the archetypal godless city, for support. The book of Isaiah itself contains a telling denouncement of Babylon in chapters 13–14. Consequently, God sends Isaiah to Hezekiah with a message:

> Hear the word of the LORD of hosts: Behold, the days are coming, when all that is in your house, and that which your fathers have stored up till this day, shall be carried to Babylon. Nothing shall be left, says the LORD. And some of your own sons, who will come from you, whom you will father, shall be taken away, and they shall be eunuchs in the palace of the king of Babylon. (Isa. 39:5–7)

Isaiah's prediction anticipates the overthrow of the Davidic dynasty by the Babylonians. This will take place in 586 BC, about a hundred years after the death of Hezekiah.

Isaiah 39 provides an interesting bridge between chapters 1–39 and 40–66. Whereas chapters 1–39 focus principally on eighth-century Jerusalem and the shortcomings of the Davidic monarch, chapters 40–48 center on the Babylonian exile that follows the destruction of Jerusalem and the demise of the Davidic government in 586 BC. In chapters 48–66, Isaiah looks beyond the initial restoration of Jerusalem after the Babylonian exile, predicting the divine creation of an eschatological new Jerusalem. The change in perspective between chapters 1–39 and 40–66 produces noteworthy contrasts between the two parts of the book of Isaiah. Nevertheless, both halves share much in common.

In light of the failure of the Davidic monarchy to ensure justice in Jerusalem, it is noteworthy that in Isaiah 44:28–45:13 the Persian ruler Cyrus is designated the Lord's anointed.[14] This Gentile king defeats the Babylonians and is responsible for initiating the rebuilding of the temple in Jerusalem (cf. 2 Chron. 36:22–23; Ezra 1:1–8). Given the Israelite belief that the Davidic king would be a source of blessing to the nations, it is ironic that God raises up a Gentile king to begin the process of restoring the temple in Jerusalem. But Cyrus's involvement in the rebuilding of the temple and city merely anticipates a much greater achievement accomplished by another "servant."

In Isaiah, the role of Cyrus is paralleled by a nameless individual, referred to as the "servant." This person is distinguished from Cyrus, but both are chosen by the Lord (Isa. 42:1, 6; 45:4; 49:7), who takes each of them by the hand (Isa. 42:6; 45:1). Fittingly, what Cyrus does for Israel is mirrored by what the servant does for the nations.

The identity of the unnamed servant in Isaiah 40–66 has prompted much discussion. He is mentioned specifically in Isaiah 42:1–9; 49:1–7; 50:4–9; 52:13–53:12, and probably also in 61:1–3, although in this latter

---

14. See esp. Isa. 45:1; cf. Isa. 41:2–7, 25; 48:14–15.

passage the term *servant* is not used.[15] The first four passages are commonly known as the "Servant Songs," but scholars differ somewhat when defining the actual boundaries of some of these songs.

The identity of the servant is much debated, with some scholars suggesting that the designation refers to Israel as a nation and not an individual.[16] On balance, it is much more likely that the servant of Isaiah 40–66 is to be equated with the promised king of Isaiah 1–39. The designation "servant" emphasizes that this individual is obedient and loyal to God.

The anonymous servant is described in various ways within Isaiah 40–66. Some features lend weight to the idea that he is a king. First, he is endowed with God's Spirit (Isa. 42:1; 61:1), a feature that recalls how Saul and David are empowered by the Spirit when Samuel anoints them (1 Sam. 10:10–12; 16:13). A similar emphasis regarding the king's being empowered by the Spirit is highlighted in Isaiah 11:1–3. Second, the servant will bring justice to the nations of the whole earth. Isaiah 42:1–4 gives emphasis to this:

> Behold my servant, whom I uphold,
> > my chosen, in whom my soul delights;
> I have put my Spirit upon him;
> > he will bring forth justice to the nations.
> He will not cry aloud or lift up his voice,
> > or make it heard in the street;
> a bruised reed he will not break,
> > and a faintly burning wick he will not quench;
> > he will faithfully bring forth justice.
> He will not grow faint or be discouraged

---

15. Barry G. Webb, *The Message of Isaiah: On Eagles' Wings*, The Bible Speaks Today (Leicester, UK: Inter-Varsity Press, 1996), 170.

16. See G. P. Hugenberger, "The Servant of the Lord in the 'Servant Songs' of Isaiah," in *The Lord's Anointed: Interpretation of Old Testament Messianic Texts*, ed. P. E. Satterthwaite, R. S. Hess, and G. J. Wenham (Grand Rapids, MI: Baker, 1995), 105–40.

> till he has established justice in the earth;
> and the coastlands wait for his law. (Isa. 42:1–4)

This expectation not only echoes what is said of the future king in Isaiah 11:5, but also recalls how the nations will come to a renewed Jerusalem in search of justice (Isa. 2:1–5). Third, in Isaiah 49, God says, "to one deeply despised, abhorred by the nation, / the servant of rulers: / 'Kings shall see and arise; / princes, and they shall prostrate themselves; / because of the LORD, who is faithful, / the Holy One of Israel, who has chosen you'" (v. 7). These comments imply that the servant will be acknowledged as having authority over kings and princes. This expectation resembles what is said elsewhere in the traditions associated with the Davidic king; a future king will exercise earthwide dominion. Fourth, the Lord affirms in Isaiah 49:5–6 that the servant will bring divine salvation to both Israel and the nations:

> And now the LORD says,
>> he who formed me from the womb to be his servant,
> to bring Jacob back to him;
>> and that Israel might be gathered to him—
> for I am honored in the eyes of the LORD,
>> and my God has become my strength—
> he says:
> "It is too light a thing that you should be my servant
>> to raise up the tribes of Jacob
>> and to bring back the preserved of Israel;
> I will make you as a light for the nations,
>> that my salvation may reach to the end of the earth."

In this passage, the servant is clearly distinguished from the nation of Israel; he is a servant to the "tribes of Jacob." The servant will restore

Israel to the Lord and be a "light for the nations," bringing them God's salvation. Again, such expectations are elsewhere linked to the Davidic monarchy (cf. Isa. 11:10–12).

Regarding the process by which Israel will be restored, Isaiah 53 emphasizes that the servant will atone for the iniquity of others by making his life "an offering for guilt" (v. 10). Repeatedly within 53:5–12 the point is emphasized that the servant willingly bears the punishment that should fall on others. Verse 5 captures well the recurring motif within this passage: "But he was pierced for our transgressions; / he was crushed for our iniquities; / upon him was the chastisement that brought us peace, / and with his wounds we are healed." One theme dominates this passage: the servant offers his life as a sacrifice to reconcile to God those who are estranged from him. Without such reconciliation, no human could possibly reside within God's holy city.

The servant's role as an atoning sacrifice is highly significant in the light of the corruption of Jerusalem and the requirement to be holy in order to ascend the mountain of God. The future servant king will suffer and die for the benefit of others. This function takes on even greater significance when it is linked to a future Davidic monarchy. Unlike the immoral Davidic kings of the eighth century, who exploit the poor and needy, the servant king will lay down his life to atone for the sins of others.[17] The servant king's self-sacrifice is even more striking because he is designated righteous by God (Isa. 53:11; cf. v. 9).

The actions of the servant are vital for the transformation of corrupt Jerusalem into a radically new city. This is underscored by the fact that the Servant Songs in chapters 49–53 are interspersed with passages that focus on the transformation of Zion.[18]

---

17. Sacrificial forgiveness is effectual only for those who confess their sin. For this reason, the wicked must "forsake his way, and the unrighteous man his thoughts" (Isa. 55:7; cf. 1:19–20).

18. See Hoppe, *The Holy City*, 104–10.

The servant's role in securing atonement for those who will live in the future Zion is also mentioned in Isaiah 61:1–3. While this passage does not explicitly refer to the speaker as either a servant or a king, the fact that he is anointed by the Lord and empowered by God's Spirit strongly suggests that these words are placed on the lips of the servant king:

> The Spirit of the Lord God is upon me,
>> because the Lord has anointed me
> to bring good news to the poor;
>> he has sent me to bind up the brokenhearted,
> to proclaim liberty to the captives,
>> and the opening of the prison to those who are bound;
> to proclaim the year of the Lord's favor,
>> and the day of vengeance of our God;
>> to comfort all who mourn;
> to grant to those who mourn in Zion—
>> to give them a beautiful headdress instead of ashes,
> the oil of gladness instead of mourning,
>> the garment of praise instead of a faint spirit;
> that they may be called oaks of righteousness,
>> the planting of the Lord, that he may be glorified.
>>> (Isa. 61:1–3)

This speech, which emphasizes themes of restoration and liberty, recalls how the book of Leviticus legislates for the Year of Jubilee (Lev. 25:8–55). The promise of liberty anticipates a radical transformation for those who have been enslaved. The oppressed will be set free, and Zion will be renewed.

By linking the unnamed servant in the second half of Isaiah to the promised future Davidic king of the first half of Isaiah, the entire book reveals that this individual will exercise a crucial role in bringing about the transformation of Jerusalem. The renewing of the corrupt city is tied to the coming of a promised righteous king. This servant king, however, does not merely bring salvation to Israel; importantly, he is also a "light for the nations" (Isa. 42:6; 49:6), mediating God's blessing to the nations in fulfillment of the promises to the patriarchs, Abraham, Isaac, and Jacob. Ultimately, his actions will result in the "glorification of God and Zion," a major theme in Isaiah 58–66.[19]

A Second Exodus

Although a major aspect of Isaiah's message involves a strident denunciation of Jerusalem's leadership for failing to trust and obey the Lord, which will lead eventually to exile in Babylon, Isaiah also brings a message of comfort from God. Using imagery that echoes the divine redemption of the Israelites from slavery in Egypt, Isaiah speaks confidently of a future return from captivity.

Isaiah inspires hope through a positive picture of a new exodus, but the description itself strongly suggests that the outcome of this future return will far exceed anything experienced in Jerusalem prior to its destruction by the Babylonians. Isaiah's words indicate that the future exodus will entail considerably more than the reinstatement of Jerusalem to its preexilic state as the capital of the kingdom of Judah and home to a restored Davidic dynasty. We see this reflected, for example, in Isaiah 35:

> The wilderness and the dry land shall be glad;
>   the desert shall rejoice and blossom like the crocus. . . .
> Strengthen the weak hands,
>   and make firm the feeble knees.
> Say to those who have an anxious heart,

19. Richard L. Schultz, "Isaiah, Book of," in *Dictionary for Theological Interpretation of the Bible*, ed. K. J. Vanhoozer, et al. (Grand Rapids, MI: Baker Academic, 2005), 341.

"Be strong; fear not!
Behold, your God
    will come with vengeance,
with the recompense of God.
    He will come and save you."

Then the eyes of the blind shall be opened,
    and the ears of the deaf unstopped;
then shall the lame man leap like a deer,
    and the tongue of the mute sing for joy.
For waters break forth in the wilderness,
    and streams in the desert. . . .

And the ransomed of the LORD shall return
    and come to Zion with singing;
everlasting joy shall be upon their heads;
    they shall obtain gladness and joy,
    and sorrow and sighing shall flee away. (Isa. 35:1,
        3–6, 10)

Remarkably, this description goes far beyond anything normally associated with exiles returning to their native land. The blind will see, the deaf will hear, and the mute tongue will shout for joy. And they will experience "everlasting joy." This is hardly to be treated as merely exaggerated language. More likely, Isaiah describes here the real experience of those who will enter the eschatological new Jerusalem.

These and other extraordinary expressions of hope scattered throughout the book of Isaiah are important. The book of Isaiah radiates a confidence that in spite of the abject failure of eighth-century Jerusalem to be the city of God, the Lord will accomplish his plan to construct a remarkable city where in the future he will dwell in harmony with humanity.

By looking beyond the corrupt Jerusalem of his day to an eschatological city, Isaiah offers hope to those who are the victims of oppression and evil. While this new Jerusalem is placed chronologically in the distant future, there are grounds for believing that Isaiah sees this eschatological city as the afterlife destiny for the righteous of his day. This is hinted at in chapter 26, where verse 19 speaks of a resurrection of the dead:[20] "Your dead shall live; their bodies shall rise. / You who dwell in the dust, awake and sing for joy! / For your dew is a dew of light, / and the earth will give birth to the dead." Interestingly, this statement comes at the end of a passage that records what people will sing in the future. The song begins with these words:

> We have a strong city;
>> he sets up salvation
>> as walls and bulwarks.
> Open the gates,
>> that the righteous nation that keeps faith may enter in.
> You keep him in perfect peace
>> whose mind is stayed on you,
>> because he trusts in you.
> Trust in the LORD forever,
>> for the LORD GOD is an everlasting rock. (Isa. 26:1–4)

It is surely significant that this song about a strong city, associated with "prefect peace,"[21] speaks of resurrection.

Isaiah undoubtedly believes in life after death. We see this reflected in a very different passage that describes the fate of the king of Babylon,

---

20. Philip C. Schmitz, "The Grammar of Resurrection in Isaiah 26:19a–c," *JBL* 122 (2003): 149, writes, "Isa 26 19b is a statement concerning the condition in which the newly reconstituted dead begin their transition to life again. The dead arise as corpses, awaken, and shout for joy. Ezekiel 37 1–14 implies similar staging of the reanimation process, and postbiblical descriptions of resurrection elaborate individual steps in the sequence."

21. "Perfect peace" translates the Hebrew expression *shālôm shālôm*.

the archetypal wicked human. Isaiah 14 records how those who have been rescued by God take up a taunt against the tyrannical king:

> How the oppressor has ceased,
>> the insolent fury ceased!
> The Lord has broken the staff of the wicked,
>> the scepter of rulers,
> that struck the peoples in wrath
>> with unceasing blows,
> that ruled the nations in anger
>> with unrelenting persecution. (Isa. 14:4–6)

Even the cedars of Lebanon rejoice, for they will no longer be felled for the benefit of the king of Babylon (Isa. 14:7–8). The scene then switches to the realm of the dead:

> Sheol beneath is stirred up
>> to meet you when you come;
> it rouses the shades to greet you,
>> all who were leaders of the earth;
> it raises from their thrones
>> all who were kings of the nations.
> All of them will answer
>> and say to you:
> "You too have become as weak as we!
>> You have become like us!"
> Your pomp is brought down to Sheol,
>> the sound of your harps;
> maggots are laid as a bed beneath you,
>> and worms are your covers. (Isa. 14:9–11)

Those in the realm of the dead then speak of how the king of Babylon has been brought low:

How you are fallen from heaven,
    O Day Star, son of Dawn!
How you are cut down to the ground,
    you who laid the nations low!
You said in your heart,
    "I will ascend to heaven;
above the stars of God
    I will set my throne on high;
I will sit on the mount of assembly
    in the far reaches of the north;
I will ascend above the heights of the clouds;
    I will make myself like the Most High."
But you are brought down to Sheol,
    to the far reaches of the pit.
Those who see you will stare at you
    and ponder over you:
"Is this the man who made the earth tremble,
    who shook kingdoms,
who made the world like a desert
    and overthrew its cities,
    who did not let his prisoners go home?"
        (Isa. 14:12–17)

This passage is sometimes mistakenly interpreted as referring to the downfall of Satan. It describes, rather, how the king of Babylon aspired to be a god, using his power to subdue nations with relentless aggression. But all his effort has not saved him from the shame of being brought down to the realm of the dead. For him there is no *shālôm*. The fate of the arrogant king of Babylon illustrates well what Isaiah states briefly elsewhere: "There is no peace [*shalom*] . . . for the wicked" (Isa. 48:22; 57:21).

This contrasts with Isaiah's expectations regarding the righteous. At the start of chapter 57, Isaiah affirms:

> The righteous man perishes,
>> and no one lays it to heart;
> devout men are taken away,
>> while no one understands.
> For the righteous man is taken away from calamity;
>> he enters into peace;
> they rest in their beds
>> who walk in their uprightness. (Isa. 57:1–2)

Isaiah speaks there of the death of the righteous. The NIV translation conveys better the sense of verse 2: "Those who walk uprightly enter into peace; they find rest as they lie in death" (cf. NLT, which reads: "Good people pass away; / the godly often die before their time. / But no one seems to care or wonder why. / No one seems to understand / that God is protecting them from the evil to come. / For those who follow godly paths / will rest in peace when they die.")

While we often speak of someone resting in peace, it is noteworthy that the Hebrew term for peace, *shālôm*, most frequently has the sense of being in a state of personal well-being, a state of health and prosperity. Isaiah can hardly be saying here that someone who becomes a lifeless corpse enters *shālôm*. More likely, the prophet envisages the righteous entering the new Jerusalem, which he associates with God coming to dwell on a renewed earth. This belief is tied to his expectation that the corrupt city of Jerusalem of his day will be transformed by God to become a metropolis of eternal *shālôm*.

Conclusion

The theme of Jerusalem transformed unifies the book of Isaiah. Looking to the future, Isaiah foresees judgment, exile, and restoration.

Through this process, God will through time change the corrupt city of Isaiah's day into a unique holy city centered on Mount Zion. Envisaging two periods of restoration, Isaiah predicts that first, Cyrus, a Gentile king, will serve as God's anointed king for the benefit of exiled Judeans. After this, an even greater "servant king" will bring salvation to Israel and the nations, preparing the way for the ultimate establishment of a cosmopolitan new Jerusalem. According to Schultz, Isaiah 40–48 anticipates a restoration of Jerusalem under the Persian king Cyrus, whereas, looking well beyond this event, Isaiah 49–57 anticipates a greater restoration of the city involving the "servant," which will lead to Zion being glorified as the ultimate city of God (Isaiah 58–66).[22]

For the first postexilic readers of Isaiah, the return from exile under Cyrus would have given them confidence to believe that God would bring to fulfillment the eschatological transformation of Jerusalem. For this reason, Isaiah's vision of an extraordinary future was not rejected in the postexilic period as merely expressing wishful, unfulfilled hopes. Rather, it was retained and prized as a genuine expectation of what God would yet accomplish in the "latter days" (Isa. 2:2). The formation of a resplendent city of God on a re-created earth was central to their eschatological hope. Moreover, the citizens of this eschatological city would include the righteous who had already died, for they would joyfully be resurrected to experience life in all its fullness.

---

22. Cf. Schultz, "Isaiah, Book of," 341.

6

Hope for Jerusalem beyond Divine Judgment

The books from Genesis to Kings record the gradual process by which God works to create a temple-city on the earth. This moves to a climax when David captures Jerusalem, and his son Solomon constructs there a permanent earthly residence for God. With the Lord present in Jerusalem, Mount Zion becomes his holy mountain abode. From his temple palace God reigns as supreme King, delegating responsibility to the Davidic monarch to be his vice-regent. The convergence of city, temple, and monarchy sets Jerusalem/Mount Zion apart from every other earthly location.

Yet the establishment of ancient Jerusalem as the city of God merely foreshadows something more marvelous to come. Beyond the reigns of David and Solomon, Jerusalem's story is marked by degeneration over time as the majority of Davidic kings and their subjects abandon allegiance to the Lord. Although God remained patient in his dealing with the population of Jerusalem, their waywardness eventually resulted in their punishment when the city was sacked by the Babylonians in 586 BC. The resulting exile fulfilled the covenantal curses recorded in Deuteronomy 28:15–68, especially verses 63–68.

The Babylonian decimation of the temple-city raised profound questions regarding God's ongoing relationship with those who survived the prolonged and horrendous siege of Jerusalem. Did the downfall of the city mark the end of God's relationship with its people? The prophetic book of Habakkuk addresses this question in a striking manner.

The Righteous Shall Live by Faith

The book of Isaiah is not alone in anticipating the destruction of Jerusalem by the Babylonians. Without specifically mentioning Jerusalem or Mount Zion, the short prophetic book of Habakkuk, composed toward the end of the seventh century BC, explores the moral appropriateness of God's using the Babylonians to punish the wayward people of Jerusalem.

Troubled by the injustice and violence that surrounds him, Habakkuk confronts God. By claiming that "the law is paralyzed, / and justice never goes forth" (Hab. 1:4), Habakkuk clearly condemns those in authority in Jerusalem, without naming the Davidic dynasty. Habakkuk's opening complaint points to the failure of the city of God to be the holy mountain associated with righteousness and peace.

In response to Habakkuk's cry for help, God reveals that he is going to raise up the Chaldeans (Babylonians) to punish the wicked. God vividly describes the Babylonians as an unstoppable force sweeping across the earth and capturing cities with ease:

> For behold, I am raising up the Chaldeans,
> that bitter and hasty nation,
> who march through the breadth of the earth,

to seize dwellings not their own.
They are dreaded and fearsome;
> their justice and dignity go forth from themselves.
Their horses are swifter than leopards,
> more fierce than the evening wolves;
> their horsemen press proudly on.
Their horsemen come from afar;
> they fly like an eagle swift to devour.
They all come for violence,
> all their faces forward.
> They gather captives like sand.
At kings they scoff,
> and at rulers they laugh.
They laugh at every fortress,
> for they pile up earth and take it.
Then they sweep by like the wind and go on,
> guilty men, whose own might is their god! (Hab. 1:6–11)

On learning of the Babylonian assault, Habakkuk asks, how can God use wicked people to punish those who are, relatively speaking, more righteous?

Graciously responding to Habakkuk, God begins by underscoring that the righteous shall live by faith (Hab. 2:4). Habakkuk 2:6–20 then records a series of woes that reveal how God will ultimately punish the Babylonians for relying upon their military might. Interestingly, two of the woes address both house and city building respectively (Hab. 2:9–14), underlining that when such structures are founded upon violence and extortion, they will not last. Responding to these reassurances, Habakkuk foresees that in the future God's glory will cover the earth as the waters cover the sea (Hab. 2:14).

Recognizing the sovereignty of God and his majestic power,

Habakkuk composes a song that ends by expressing incredible hope in God. Acknowledging that times of extreme difficulty may come, Habakkuk asserts his confidence in God, using imagery related to standing on a mountain.

> Though the fig tree should not blossom,
>   nor fruit be on the vines,
> the produce of the olive fail
>   and the fields yield no food,
> the flock be cut off from the fold
>   and there be no herd in the stalls,
> yet I will rejoice in the LORD;
>   I will take joy in the God of my salvation.
> GOD, the Lord, is my strength;
>   he makes my feet like the deer's;
>   he makes me tread on my high places. (Hab. 3:17–19)

The overall message of the book of Habakkuk implies that those who have faith in God will look beyond the destruction of Jerusalem by the Babylonians. Their faith in God will give them confidence that God's glory will ultimately fill the whole earth and that those who trust in him will be protected.

Jeremiah's Warning against a False Confidence in Jerusalem

Habakkuk is not alone in predicting that God will use the Babylonians to punish the people of Jerusalem. The theme of divine judgment figures prominently in the book of Jeremiah. Like Habakkuk, Jeremiah predicts the overthrow of Jerusalem by the Babylonians but emphasizes surprisingly that Judeans exiled to Babylon are to be considered fortunate, compared to those left in Jerusalem. Although the theme of imminent judgment is dominant, Jeremiah also offers hope regarding the future of Jerusalem.

Born around 650 BC, Jeremiah grew up a few miles from Jerusalem in the town of Anathoth. In the thirteenth year of King Josiah (628/627 BC), God summoned Jeremiah, the son of a priest, to be a prophet. Jeremiah's subsequent ministry straddled several decades up to the fall of Jerusalem in 586 BC and for a few years afterward. The book that bears his name consists largely of prophetic messages for the people of Jerusalem and Judah, calling on them to repent. However, Jeremiah also addresses other nations (Jeremiah 46–51). His oracles are occasionally interspersed with biographical information about Jeremiah's activity as a prophet.

Jeremiah spoke out against the idolatry of those living in Jerusalem (e.g., Jer. 2:18–19). He also denounced those who mistakenly believed that the temple's presence in Jerusalem guaranteed them divine protection and security (Jer. 7:4, 14).[1] Mistakenly, the people placed their trust in the temple building and not in its extraordinary resident. Although Jeremiah refers to God's earlier abandonment of the temple in Shiloh (Jer. 7:3–15; 26:4–6), he did not believe that Jerusalem would be abandoned forever.

Jeremiah faced opposition from false prophets who predicted an imminent return for those already taken to Babylon (Jer. 27:16). In contrast, Jeremiah spoke of seventy years of Babylonian supremacy (Jer. 25:11; cf. 29:10) and invited those Judeans exiled in Babylon to seek the welfare of the city.[2] While exile from Jerusalem was not normally something to be welcomed, it was safer to be in Babylon, away from Jerusalem. And those exiled were encouraged by Jeremiah to wait patiently for God's restoration of the city.

---

1. Cf. G. K. Beale and Mitchell Kim, *God Dwells among Us: Expanding Eden to the Ends of the Earth* (Downers Grove, IL: InterVarsity, 2014), 65.

2. Although it is often said that Jeremiah predicted seventy years of exile for the people of Jerusalem, the period between the fall of Jerusalem in 586 BC and the return of exiles in 538 BC is only forty-four years. The wording of Jer. 25:11 indicates that the seventy years refers to events that include other nations: "This whole land shall become a ruin and a waste, and these nations shall serve the king of Babylon seventy years" (Jer. 25:11).

To illustrate to Jeremiah the contrasting situations of the Judeans in Jerusalem and in Babylon, God uses two baskets of figs that are placed before the temple. "One basket had very good figs, like first-ripe figs, but the other basket had very bad figs, so bad that they could not be eaten" (Jer. 24:2). God compares the basket of good figs to the Judean exiles in Babylon, promising that he will bring them back to Jerusalem (vv. 5–6). Reassuringly, God emphasises that they shall be his people and he will be their God (v. 7). In marked contrast, the basket of bad figs represents "Zedekiah the king of Judah, his officials, the remnant of Jerusalem who remain in this land, and those who dwell in the land of Egypt" (v. 8). God condemns them to be punished by "sword, famine, and pestilence" (v. 10). The fates of the two groups could hardly be more different. Ironically, those who remained in Jerusalem arrogantly believed that they were the ones specially favored by God.

Jeremiah's letter to the Judean exiles in Babylon conveys well his optimism regarding their future well-being. He wrote:

> Thus says the LORD of hosts, the God of Israel, to all the exiles whom I have sent into exile from Jerusalem to Babylon: Build houses and live in them; plant gardens and eat their produce. Take wives and have sons and daughters; take wives for your sons, and give your daughters in marriage, that they may bear sons and daughters; multiply there, and do not decrease. But seek the welfare of the city where I have sent you into exile, and pray to the LORD on its behalf, for in its welfare you will find your welfare. (Jer. 29:4–7)

Jeremiah then goes on to say that after seventy years God will bring the people back to Jerusalem.

Jeremiah's message that God would use the Babylonians to punish the wayward people of Jerusalem was not received favorably by the people living in Judah, especially those in positions of authority. Some of his prophetic oracles, which would have sounded pro-Babylonian,[3] were perceived as being less than patriotic. In the tense environment of Jerusalem being threatened by Babylon, Jeremiah was threatened with death (Jer. 26:1–24) and imprisoned for a time within Jerusalem (Jer. 37:1–21). There were even those who attempted to end his life (Jer. 38:1–13).

While Jeremiah was adamant that the Babylonians would execute judgment on God's behalf against the people of Jerusalem, he was equally confident that Babylon itself would ultimately come under God's judgment (cf. Jer. 50:1–51:64). As Arnold notes:

> Babylon, the great conqueror of all nations will itself be conquered, and like Isaiah's prophecy, Jeremiah anticipates a day when Babylon will become an utter desolation, unfit for human occupation (Jer 50:3, 13; 51:29, 37). Indeed, Babylon will become like Sodom and Gomorrah, uninhabitable (Jer 50:39–40; cf. Is 13:19). And again like Isaiah, Jeremiah identifies the Medes as Babylon's destroyer (Jer 51:11, 28).[4]

The interaction between Jerusalem and Babylon takes on added significance when we recall how Babylon is perceived throughout the Bible as the archetypal godless city.

Although Jeremiah warned the people of Jerusalem to turn from their evil ways, his call to repent fell on deaf ears. Nevertheless, while Jerusalem would fall to the Babylonians, Jeremiah anticipated that a righteous remnant of Judeans would survive and return

---

3. As J. R. Soza, "Jeremiah," in *New Dictionary of Biblical Theology*, ed. T. D. Alexander and B. S. Rosner (Leicester, UK: Inter-Varsity, 2000), 226–27, observes, "The prophet celebrates Babylon as God's instrument of judgment (chs. 46–49)."

4. Bill T. Arnold, "Babylon," in *Dictionary of the Old Testament: Prophets*, ed. M. J. Boda and J. G. McConville (Downers Grove, IL: IVP Academic, 2012), 57.

to Jerusalem. He saw "in the divine purpose more than retribution, rather, authentic restoration."[5] Consequently, amid the biographical details recorded in the book, we are told that Jeremiah purchased land in Jerusalem to signal his confidence in God's commitment to the city (Jer. 32:7–12). Later, when Jeremiah was offered asylum in Babylon (Jer. 40:1–6), he chose to remain in Jerusalem. And when he was eventually taken to Egypt against his will, he warned against the danger of seeking refuge there (Jer. 42:9–43:7).

Looking to the future, Jeremiah foresaw that Jerusalem would be restored as the city of God. However, he indicated that the old covenant inaugurated at Mount Sinai would be replaced by a new covenant that would involve God's law being inscribed on human hearts (Jer. 31:32–33).This transformation would herald a new age for Jerusalem. As Thomas observes:

> The theme of safety and security of Zion after judgment permeates Jeremiah 32–33. This is combined with an inward fidelity to the Lord, depicted in God's writing of the law on the hearts of the faithful (Jer 31:33–34). In this divinely orchestrated "restoration of fortunes" (cf. Jer 31:23; 32:44; 33:7, 11, 26), God will instill within Zion fidelity, love and faithfulness not known before in Israel's history. What is called upon for the faithful of God is to await this divinely orchestrated change in penitence, faith and confident expectancy.[6]

While Jeremiah was adamant that Jerusalem would fall to the Babylonians, he did not consider this event as marking the end of God's dealings with the citizens of Jerusalem. There would be restoration immediately after the Babylonian exile, but Jeremiah antici-

---

5. Leslie J. Hoppe, *The Holy City: Jerusalem in the Theology of the Old Testament* (Collegeville, MN: Liturgical Press, 2000), 87.

6. H. A. Thomas, "Zion," in *Dictionary of the Old Testament: Prophets*, ed. M. J. Boda and J. G. McConville (Downers Grove, IL: IVP Academic, 2012), 911.

pates a wonderful renewal that goes far beyond what happened in the late fifth and early fourth centuries BC (cf. Jer. 3:17).

Daniel: A Babylonian Perspective on Jerusalem's Future

Jeremiah's expectations that Judean exiles would be protected by God in Babylon are reflected in the book of Daniel. This distinct Old Testament book, half written in Hebrew and half in Aramaic, describes the experiences in Babylon of four Judean exiles: Daniel, Shadrach, Meshach, and Abednego. Their desire to remain loyal to the Lord God and his covenant obligations quickly brings them into conflict with Nebuchadnezzar, king of Babylon. In the opening chapter of Daniel, the four young men refuse to defile themselves by taking "the king's food" and "the wine that he drank" (Dan. 1:8). Preferring to eat only vegetables and drink only water, after a ten-day trial they appear healthier and better nourished than those who ate the royal food. God rewards their loyalty by giving them "learning and skill in all literature and wisdom," and he also endows Daniel with the ability to understand visions and dreams of all kinds (Dan. 1:17). When eventually Nebuchadnezzar examines them, he finds them "ten times better than all the magicians and enchanters that were in all his kingdom" (Dan. 1:20).

After this, Nebuchadnezzar has a dream in which he sees a great image with a head of gold, chest and arms of silver, a middle and thighs of bronze, legs of iron, and feet partly of iron and partly of clay (Dan. 2:31–33). As Nebuchadnezzar watches, a stone strikes the image, destroying it completely. Finally the stone becomes "a great mountain" and fills the whole earth (Dan. 2:35). When Nebuchadnezzar challenges the "wise men of Babylon" to tell his dream, only Daniel has the ability to recount its contents.

When Daniel interprets the dream for Nebuchadnezzar, he reveals that it describes four consecutive human kingdoms, of which Nebuchadnezzar's is the first. Eventually these kingdoms are destroyed when the God of heaven sets up a new kingdom. In light of Daniel's Judean origin, the idea that the kingdom of God is symbolized by a rock that becomes a huge mountain, filling the whole earth, recalls prophetic expectations associated with Mount Zion. As a consequence of interpreting the dream for Nebuchadnezzar, Daniel and his friends are appointed to positions of responsibility within Babylon.

God's protection of the Judean exiles is further illustrated in Daniel 3, which describes how Nebuchadnezzar makes an enormous golden image that everyone must worship. When Shadrach, Meshach, and Abednego refuse to do this, the king commands that they should be burned to death in a furnace "seven times more than it was usually heated" (Dan. 3:19). Remarkably the three men survive unharmed. When they emerge from the fire, "the hair of their heads was not singed, their cloaks were not harmed, and no smell of fire had come upon them" (Dan. 3:27). The incident impacts Nebuchadnezzar so much that he proclaims:

> Blessed be the God of Shadrach, Meshach, and Abednego, who has sent his angel and delivered his servants, who trusted in him, and set aside the king's command, and yielded up their bodies rather than serve and worship any god except their own God. Therefore I make a decree: Any people, nation, or language that speaks anything against the God of Shadrach, Meshach, and Abednego shall be torn limb from limb, and their houses laid in ruins, for there is no other god who is able to rescue in this way. (Dan. 3:28–29)

In these and other ways, the book of Daniel illustrates how God protected and promoted the Judean exiles even when they were forced to live within the archetypal godless city of Babylon.

In addition, their presence in Babylon enables them to witness to others regarding God's sovereignty over heaven and earth. When Daniel graciously interprets for Nebuchadnezzar a dream involving a great tree, he highlights how the Babylonian king will be humbled by God. Daniel warns Nebuchadnezzar that God will make him like one of the "beasts of the field," eating "grass like an ox" (Dan. 4:25). In the light of this warning, Daniel counsels the king to show mercy to the oppressed (Dan. 4:27).

When twelve months later Nebuchadnezzar proudly boasts, "Is not this great Babylon, which I have built by my mighty power as a royal residence and for the glory of my majesty?" (Dan. 4:30), a voice from heaven announces that he will be driven away from people and will live with the wild animals. After some time, humbled by his experience, Nebuchadnezzar acknowledges and praises the Most High. He tells his subjects:

> At the end of the days I, Nebuchadnezzar, lifted my eyes to heaven, and my reason returned to me, and I blessed the Most High, and praised and honored him who lives forever,
>
> > for his dominion is an everlasting dominion,
> > > and his kingdom endures from generation to generation;
> > all the inhabitants of the earth are accounted as nothing,
> > > and he does according to his will among the host of heaven
> > and among the inhabitants of the earth;
> > and none can stay his hand
> > > or say to him, "What have you done?"
> > > > (Dan. 4:34–35)

Against the background of Nebuchadnezzar's army sacking Jerusalem and destroying the temple, the stories recorded in the book of Daniel are noteworthy for illustrating God's remarkable protection of Judean exiles in Babylon. They are very much in keeping with the positive sentiments expressed by Jeremiah concerning those taken away from Jerusalem by the Babylonians.

Furthermore, running as a major theme throughout the book of Daniel is the expectation that beyond this time of exile God will renew Jerusalem. While different chapters in the book of Daniel foretell in a variety of ways how God's kingdom will eclipse all other kingdoms,[7] Daniel 9 is especially interesting because it begins by alluding directly to Jeremiah's mention of seventy years.

> In the first year of Darius the son of Ahasuerus, by descent a Mede, who was made king over the realm of the Chaldeans—in the first year of his reign, I, Daniel, perceived in the books the number of years that, according to the word of the LORD to Jeremiah the prophet, must pass before the end of the desolations of Jerusalem, namely, seventy years. (Dan. 9:1–2)

This hope leads Daniel to pray passionately for the restoration of Jerusalem. Though his prayer is dominated by Daniel identifying with his fellow Judeans and confessing his and their rebellious wrongdoing, it concludes with a series of exodus petitions focused almost exclusively on Jerusalem:

> O Lord, according to all your righteous acts, let your anger and your wrath turn away from your city Jerusalem, your holy hill, because for our sins, and for the iniquities of our

---

7. The visions in Daniel 2 and 7 provide excellent examples of this.

fathers, Jerusalem and your people have become a byword among all who are around us. Now therefore, O our God, listen to the prayer of your servant and to his pleas for mercy, and for your own sake, O Lord, make your face to shine upon your sanctuary, which is desolate. O my God, incline your ear and hear. Open your eyes and see our desolations, and the city that is called by your name. For we do not present our pleas before you because of our righteousness, but because of your great mercy. O Lord, hear; O Lord, forgive. O Lord, pay attention and act. Delay not, for your own sake, O my God, because your city and your people are called by your name. (Dan. 9:16–19)

With passion Daniel expresses his longing for the restoration of Jerusalem, God's "holy hill."

Fittingly, God responds, giving Daniel a somewhat cryptic message regarding the future (Dan. 9:24–27). Although the precise meaning of this divine message is much debated, especially regarding the significance of the seventy weeks, it implies that Jerusalem will continue to play a role in the outworking of God's purposes for the world.

God's Anger toward Jerusalem

If the book of Daniel conveys something of God's protection of those in exile in Babylon, the book of Lamentations in marked contrast graphically describes the horror that befell those in Jerusalem. In a series of alphabetic acrostics, Lamentations conveys the painful consequences of divine anger. No effort is made to sanitize what God did to Jerusalem. No attempt is made to shift the blame to the Babylonians for the terrible suffering inflicted upon the city's population. With exceptional literary skill, the author of

Lamentations expresses with vivid images the experience of being the target of divine retribution. The anguish of what took place permeates the entire book, and nowhere is this more evident than in the opening stanzas of chapter 3. With frightening honesty, the author vividly describes at length how it feels to be attacked by God (Lam. 3:1–20). The tone of the whole passage is captured well in its opening words:

> I am the man who has seen affliction
>> under the rod of his wrath;
> he has driven and brought me
>> into darkness without any light;
> surely against me he turns his hand
>> again and again the whole day long. (Lam. 3:1–3)

A more harrowing description of divine anger cannot be found in the Bible. In light of such a personal attack, it is no surprise that those who survived the siege of Jerusalem felt totally alienated from God. What hope could they possibly have?

Yet, against the blackest of backgrounds, the sufferer in Lamentations 3 unexpectedly looks up with hope. As if from nowhere, he announces:

> But this I call to mind,
>> and therefore I have hope:
>
> The steadfast love of the Lord never ceases;
>> his mercies never come to an end;
> they are new every morning;
>> great is your faithfulness.
> "The Lord is my portion," says my soul,
>> "therefore I will hope in him."

The LORD is good to those who wait for him,
>to the soul who seeks him.
It is good that one should wait quietly
>for the salvation of the LORD.
It is good for a man that he bear
>the yoke in his youth.

Let him sit alone in silence
>when it is laid on him;
let him put his mouth in the dust—
>there may yet be hope;
let him give his cheek to the one who strikes,
>and let him be filled with insults.

For the Lord will not
>cast off forever,
but, though he cause grief, he will have compassion
>according to the abundance of his steadfast love;
for he does not afflict from his heart
>or grieve the children of men. (Lam. 3:21–33; cf.
>>Hos. 6:1)

Those targeted by divine anger cannot presume upon the grace of God, but the prior experiences of the Israelites gave them grounds for believing that reconciliation with God was still possible.[8]

Expressions of hope sparkle in other Old Testament sources associated with the exilic period. However, as is evident in the oracles of Isaiah and other prophets, hope for the future was not focused on the renewal of Jerusalem to its preexilic state. Something much more

---

8. Ex. 34:6–7 provides an important summary of God's forgiving nature that becomes a central component of Israelite faith (cf. Num. 14:18; Neh. 9:17; Pss. 86:15; 103:8; 145:8; Joel 2:13; Jonah 4:2) and is alluded to elsewhere (e.g., 2 Chron. 30:9; Neh. 9:31; Pss. 111:4; 112:4; Jer. 32:18; Nah. 1:3)

significant was anticipated, still centered on God's desire to dwell in harmony with humanity on the earth.

Ezekiel's Visions of God Abandoning and Returning to Jerusalem

Among the citizens of Judah for whom Isaiah's vision of a new Jerusalem might have offered comfort was the prophet Ezekiel, a younger contemporary of Jeremiah. Born into a priestly family toward the end of the seventh century BC, Ezekiel expected at the age of thirty to be consecrated for ministry within the Jerusalem temple. However, in 597 BC, when he was twenty-five years old, Ezekiel was deported, along with others, from Judah to Babylonia. At thirty years of age, the age for temple service, Ezekiel had the first of various visions through which God spoke to him. Further visions came to him over the next twenty years.

Little would have prepared Ezekiel for his first vision, when he witnesses the awe-inspiring chariot throne of God coming to him in southern Mesopotamia. Ezekiel would have associated the glory of God with the Most Holy Place inside the Jerusalem temple. To Ezekiel's surprise, the Lord appears to him in Babylonia. This extraordinary vision signaled loudly that the sovereign Lord had not forsaken his people in Babylonia. Exile from Jerusalem did not mean abandonment by God.

The initial messages communicated to Ezekiel highlight God's dismay and anger at the corruption evident within Jerusalem. This is especially evident in Ezekiel 5:5–12, where God denounces Jerusalem for its wickedness. As a righteous judge, God reveals plainly to Ezekiel that the rebellious population of Jerusalem will be punished for defiling the temple-city.

Subsequent revelations to Ezekiel confirm that Jerusalem and its temple will soon be demolished. Transported in a vision to the

Jerusalem temple, Ezekiel witnesses a variety of idolatrous activities that desecrate the temple (Ezek. 8:3–16). In light of these, God warns Ezekiel that these "great abominations" committed by the house of Israel are driving him from his sanctuary (Ezek. 8:6). Ezekiel then witnesses "the glory of the God of Israel" depart from the temple (Ezek. 9:3). Due to the people's sins, God leaves the city. As God reveals to Ezekiel, "The guilt of the house of Israel and Judah is exceedingly great. The land is full of blood, and the city full of injustice. For they say, 'The LORD has forsaken the land, and the LORD does not see'" (Ezek. 9:9).

Tellingly, chapters 8–11 of Ezekiel reveal that God is reticent to abandon the temple and Jerusalem. Commenting on Ezekiel 10, Taylor observes that God's departure "was only a partial departure: from inner sanctum to threshold, as if the LORD is reluctant to leave and is almost pressurized into moving further away from the idolatrous epicentre that was once his dwelling place."[9] Ezekiel 11:23 describes how God moves "from the midst of the city" to a "mountain that is on the east side of the city." The Lord then looks over the city with regret.

Ezekiel's vision of the divine abandonment of Jerusalem makes clear that the Babylonian destruction of the temple in 586 BC is not a consequence of God's failure to defend his temple-city. God himself determines what occurs; he forsakes the temple due to the people's idolatry and injustice, as Jerusalem comes under severe judgment.

In subsequent visions, Ezekiel discovers that in spite of the severity of God's anger against the people of Jerusalem, God has not abandoned his plans to create on the earth a temple-city. While a variety of passages in Ezekiel look with confidence to the future, the hope of a new beginning is most graphically conveyed through Ezekiel's vision of the valley of dry bones (Ezek. 37:1–14). The restoration of

---

9. J. B. Taylor, "The Temple in Ezekiel," in *Heaven on Earth: The Temple in Biblical Theology,* ed. T. D. Alexander and S. Gathercole (Carlisle, UK: Paternoster, 2004), 67.

life to these long-dead corpses points emphatically toward a new beginning. And as Ezekiel 37 goes on to reveal, this new start will entail a restoration of city, temple, and monarchy:

> My servant David shall be king over them, and they shall all have one shepherd. They shall walk in my rules and be careful to obey my statutes. They shall dwell in the land that I gave to my servant Jacob, where your fathers lived. They and their children and their children's children shall dwell there forever, and David my servant shall be their prince forever. I will make a covenant of peace with them. It shall be an everlasting covenant with them. And I will set them in their land and multiply them, and will set my sanctuary in their midst forevermore. My dwelling place shall be with them, and I will be their God, and they shall be my people. Then the nations will know that I am the Lord who sanctifies Israel, when my sanctuary is in their midst forevermore. (Ezek. 37:24–28)

Like Isaiah, Ezekiel associates the creation of the ideal Jerusalem with the activity of a future Davidic king. Since the origin of Jerusalem as the "city of God" is linked to David's capture of the city from the Jebusites, it is most appropriate that the creation of a new Jerusalem should also involve a Davidic king. As McConville notes:

> The promise of the exiles' return to the "high mountain of Israel" (Ezekiel's typical way of referring to Jerusalem) is associated with the expectation of a renewed Davidic monarchy. In 17:22–24, such a scenario follows upon the fall of Babylon. . . . David will be Yahweh's "shepherd" . . . ; he will rule over a unified nation, a "prince for ever," Yahweh's sanctuary being in the midst of the people (37:22–26). . . . The message of Ezekiel seems clear: Yahweh will vindicate himself among the nations

by delivering the exiles from Babylon, and by dwelling among them in Jerusalem, with a Davidic king on the throne (see also Ezk. 36:24, 33–38).[10]

While the picture painted in Ezekiel 37 implies a restoration of what has been lost due to the sacking of Jerusalem by the Babylonians, the future described here entails much more than merely a return to the situation that existed prior to the fall of the city. This is reinforced by the visions recorded in Ezekiel 40–48.

Whereas Ezekiel 8–11 describes God's reluctant departure from the sanctuary in Jerusalem, chapters 40–48, especially chapters 43–46, focus on God's return to a new temple. This latter vision is dated to 572 BC, twenty years after Ezekiel's first vision, and fourteen years after the decimation of Jerusalem. At the time of this vision the Jerusalem temple has long been reduced to ruins. Unlike Ezekiel's earlier visions of judgment upon the idolatrous population of Jerusalem, the emphasis in chapters 40–48 is upon the return of God's glory to a renewed temple-city. This return is described most fully in chapter 43:1–9, where Ezekiel speaks of "the glory of the God of Israel . . . coming from the east" and entering the temple with the intention of living there forever. Ezekiel's vision undoubtedly anticipates God returning to dwell within the temple-city. What is less clear is the timeline for this development, especially given that the postexilic temple and city do not correspond to the description set out by Ezekiel.

Scholars debate the nature of Ezekiel's visions in chapters 40–48. The weight of evidence favors seeing Ezekiel's final vision as portraying an idealized replacement temple-city. The artificiality of the vision suggests that its contents are to be understood as emblematic.

---

10. Gordon McConville, "Jerusalem in the Old Testament," in *Jerusalem Past and Present in the Purposes of God*, ed. P. W. L. Walker (Croydon, UK: Deo Gloria Trust, 1992), 41.

Taylor sees chapters 40–48 as "idealized and essentially symbolic in character and intention."[11] A similar view is expressed by Block:

> While some elements of Ezekiel's vision of the future derive from well-known physical realities, others are quite idealistic and even unimaginable. . . . The river, whose source lies within the temple complex itself, flows through the Judean desert increasing dramatically in size, and turning the wasteland into an Edenic paradise, even healing (*rāpā'*) the Dead Sea (47:1–12). The plan of the city is idealized as a perfect square with three gates punctuating each side to provide admittance for the twelve tribes. The emphasis on the twelve tribes itself reverses five centuries of history. The apportionment of the land of Israel among the tribes to a large extent disregards topographic and historical realities. The dimensions of the temple and the city are dominated by multiples of five, with twenty-five being a particularly common number. All in all Ezekiel's scheme appears highly contrived, casting doubt on any interpretation that expects a literal fulfillment of his plan.[12]

Although Ezekiel's vision in chapters 40–48 is a highly idealized picture of the future, it communicates powerfully, like the concluding chapters of Isaiah, that God is still committed to the process of constructing a temple-city on the earth where he will dwell. As McConville notes, "Though the name Zion does not occur in the Book of Ezekiel, the Zion-tradition is central to its message. . . . The whole structure of the prophecy is built on the idea of a temporary withdrawal of Yahweh from Jerusalem, in expression of his wrath

---

11. Taylor, "The Temple in Ezekiel," 69.
12. Daniel I. Block, *The Book of Ezekiel: Chapters 25–48*, NICOT (Grand Rapids, MI: Eerdmans, 1998), 501–2.

over a corrupt people, to be followed in due course by his triumphant return."[13] Anticipating a future temple-city, Ezekiel's final vision concludes with *Yerushalayim*, "Jerusalem," being renamed *Yahweh-shammah*, "The LORD Is There" (Ezek. 48:35). No indication is given, however, as to when and how this ideal city will be established.

Ezekiel's vision of the restored Jerusalem is not a blueprint for the postexilic reconstruction of Jerusalem. It envisions so much more, for the fulfillment goes beyond what might be achieved by human efforts alone. Only a divine intervention of great magnitude could result in the kind of temple-city described by Ezekiel. While the imagery is temple orientated, Ezekiel's city resembles Isaiah's vision of a God-created new Jerusalem that is to be equated with a re-created earth. This prospect, however, remained unfulfilled in the postexilic period, even after returning exiles reconstructed the temple and repaired the walls of Jerusalem.[14]

Zechariah's Vision of a Faithful Jerusalem

Expectations regarding a future new Jerusalem are not limited merely to the prophets who lived in the second half of the seventh century BC and in the first half of the sixth century BC. The postexilic prophet Zechariah also speaks of a transformed Jerusalem where God will dwell. We see this most clearly in chapter 8, which comprises a series of short oracles about Jerusalem:

> The first oracle (v. 2) insists on God's eternal love for Jerusalem. In the second (v. 3) Zechariah coins another expression. He says that Jerusalem will be called "the city of truth" (8:3). The prophet uses this epithet to underscore the importance of a just social order in the city. . . . The third oracle (vv. 4–5)

---

13. McConville, "Jerusalem in the Old Testament," 40.
14. On the reconstruction of the temple and city walls, see the books of Ezra and Nehemiah.

paints a charming picture of Jerusalem's elderly sitting in the city's squares, while the city's children are at play, to convey the peace and prosperity that will be part of Jerusalem's future. The fourth oracle (v. 6) affirms God's power to restore the city. The passage concludes with three oracles that envision a return of exiles from the Diaspora (vv. 7–8), promise the blessings of prosperity (vv. 9–13), and call for the restoration of Jerusalem (vv. 14–15).[15]

Commenting on the expectations outlined in Zechariah 8, Gowan writes:

> The good life that Zechariah projects for the inhabitants of Jerusalem is a mixture of the material and the spiritual. Peace, prosperity, and security are dominant themes, but his is no secular city. What makes it all possible is God, who carries out his purpose (8:2, 6, 11, 13b–15), and the source of the good life in Zion is the presence of Yahweh in its midst. Zechariah 8 begins, "I will return to Zion and will dwell in the midst of Jerusalem," and it ends, "we have heard that God is with you."[16]

These future expectations were clearly intended to encourage Zechariah's contemporaries in the late sixth century BC to finish rebuilding the temple. While the completed structure was unable to match the splendor of the temple constructed by Solomon, its erection was a powerful signal that God was still concerned to fulfill his creation blueprint. The subsequent rebuilding of the walls of Jerusalem, in the

---

15. Hoppe, *The Holy City*, 118.

16. Donald E. Gowan, *Eschatology in the Old Testament* (Philadelphia: Fortress Press, 1986), 6. Anthony Petterson (*Haggai, Zechariah, and Malachi*, ApOTC 25 [Downers Grove, IL: InterVarsity Press, 2015], 205), argues persuasively that the phrase "I have returned to Zion," found also in 1:16, should be translated "I have turned to Zion," with the sense "God has turned from anger toward his people to mercy." The verse should not be taken to mean that God is already living in Zion. When this oracle was first spoken, the temple was still under construction.

face of stern opposition, further confirmed that the departure of God from Jerusalem at the start of the Babylonian exile did not mark the end of God's intention to dwell with humanity on the earth. In spite of the setbacks of the sixth century, Jerusalem and its temple still had a role to play as God continued to establish his presence throughout the world. However, going forward, the focus of attention shifts toward the future creation of a new Jerusalem that will far outshine the city restored by the returning Jewish exiles in the fifth century BC.

Conclusion

The combined witness of the Old Testament prophets of the eighth to the sixth centuries BC affirms that a new Jerusalem is central to their eschatological expectations. This is demonstrated by the number of passages in the prophetic books that anticipate a greatly transformed Zion. In all, Gowan identifies forty-three references in Isaiah, thirteen in Jeremiah, ten in Ezekiel, and eight in Zechariah.[17] These expectations envisage a city that far exceeds a restoration of Jerusalem to its preexilic state. Moreover, the language and imagery used to describe future Jerusalem strongly suggest that the astounding expectations of the prophets are linked to the idea that the whole earth will become God's temple-city through a process of re-creation. As Thomas notes:

> When the prophetic testimony on Zion is taken together, Zion becomes a witness to God's universal dominion in creation

---

17. Gowan, *Eschatology in the Old Testament*, 9, lists the following passages: Isa. 1:24–26; 2:2–4; 4:2–6; 11:6–9; 18:7; 24:21–23; 25:6–8; 26:1; 27:11; 28:16; 29:8; 30:19–26, 29; 31:4–5; 32:14–20; 33:5–6; 33:17–24; 34:8; 35:10, 37:30–32; 40:2, 9; 41:27; 44:24–28; 45:13; 46:13; 48:2; 49:14–26; 51:1–3, 9–11, 12–16; 52:1–10; 54:1–17; 56:3–8; 57:11–13; 59:20; 60:10–14; 61:1–11; 62:1–12; 65:17–25; 66:1, 6, 10–14, 18–21; Jer. 3:14–18; 27:22; 29:10–14; 30:18–22; 31:6, 10–14, 23, 38–40; 32:36–41, 44; 33:4–16; 50:4–5; Ezek. 16:59–63; 17:22–24; 20:40–44; 34:20–30; 37:24–28; 40:2; 43:12; 45:6–8; 47:1–12; 48:35; Zech. 1:14–17; 2:1–12; 3:2; 8:1–23; 9:9–10; 12:1–9; 13:1; 14:1–21. In addition, Gowan notes that "Jerusalem as the ideal city" is mentioned in Dan. 9:2, 24–26; Joel 3:17–21; Obad. 15–21; Hag. 2:9; Mic. 4:1–13; Zeph. 3:14–20; and Mal. 3:4. See W. J. Dumbrell, *The End of the Beginning: Revelation 21–22 and the Old Testament* (Grand Rapids, MI: Baker, 1985), 5–27.

(see Is 60). As a theological symbol, Zion presses the future hope well beyond any former localization in the prophets' presentation of history. Zion, then, absorbs the grandeur of Israel's Sinai theophany into a new vision of God's universal reign in creation (Levenson). Although the Zion tradition may link back to creation theology, in the prophets the vision of "restored Zion" is a picture of creation *redivivus*. . . . In this way, for the prophets Zion becomes a rich theological symbol that depicts the reign of God over his creation in time and eternity. Zion becomes a symbol of new creation and redeemed humanity that lives before God without sin, death or pain because God rules in its midst (cf. Is 2:2–4; 65; Mic 4:14).[18]

Expectations regarding the future are strongly influenced by the idea of a radically new Jerusalem. This prospect, which finds expression most strongly in the book of Isaiah, comes also in Jeremiah and Ezekiel. Similar hopes are found scattered across other prophetic books, and elsewhere. In all of this, however, a dichotomy exists between the historical Jerusalem of the postexilic period and the new Jerusalem of prophetic expectation. The hopes associated with the latter far exceed the reality of the rebuilt Jerusalem. As McConville observes:

Where "Zion" imagery is retained in expressions of hope for the future (in the post-exilic literature), it is rarely (if ever) in the form of a simple return to the *status quo ante*. The shared prophetic vision of a restored Israel is of an entity that is qualitatively different; in the terms of the New Covenant, this is based in turn on an act of God that is qualitatively dif-

18. Thomas, "Zion," 912–13.

ferent. It is not easy to turn such prophecies into a vision for the historical city of Jerusalem. This is the more true of that literature in which hopes for Jerusalem introduce an eschatological element, removing it from the ordinary historical plane. Jerusalem becomes, in the prophetic vision, a symbol of God's final work of salvation for all the nations, who unite in their knowledge and worship of him. In all this Jerusalem—the historical city—recedes into the background.[19]

The prophetic expectations linked to the new Jerusalem are not simply focused on the nation of Israel. For the prophets, future Jerusalem takes on a more universal dimension, involving the nations of the earth. Capturing something of this, Thomas writes:

> Zion as a symbol intertwines the destiny of Israel with the nations. As those who have been judged and remain, the nations and Israel will find refuge in Zion under the protection of God, the instruction of God, and his appointed king (Mic 4:1–2; Zeph 3:9; Zech 2:10–11; 8:1–23). After purification of sin, Israel and the nations are incorporated into a new humanity—ideal Israel, in Zion (Joel 2:23–32).[20]

To understand how this and other aspects of the hopes associated with Jerusalem develop, we move from the Old Testament to the New Testament.

---

19. McConville, "Jerusalem in the Old Testament," 47.
20. Thomas, "Zion," 913.

7

Seeking the City That Is to Come

In the preceding chapters we have observed how the book of Genesis commences by signaling God's intention to dwell on the earth in harmony with humanity. Tragically, the treacherous actions of Adam and Eve alienate people from God, disrupting severely God's plans for creation. In spite of all that happens, however, people retain their God-given ability to be city builders. While humans desire to usurp God's authority by creating cities over which they will rule, the Old Testament story records God's gracious and patient activity to reverse the consequences of humanity's alienation from him. In spite of human opposition, God will build his holy city on the earth.

Through the descendants of Abraham, God eventually establishes Jerusalem as a temple-city, where he dwells with his people. The inauguration of Jerusalem as the city of God is closely linked to the expectation that God's rule will extend throughout the whole earth, under the vice-regency of a Davidic king. Unfortunately, in the years following the creation of the Davidic dynasty, the citizens of Jerusalem defile the city through perverse behavior, resulting eventually in the Babylonian destruction of the city and the exiling of

God's people. Although the temple and city walls are later restored, prophetic expectations anticipate a new Jerusalem that will far exceed in magnitude and grandeur the city of Jerusalem in both the preexilic and postexilic periods. The realization of these hopes rests on the coming of a new Davidic king, who will serve as a true vice-regent of the Lord, establishing God's kingdom throughout the earth.

In light of these expectations, the New Testament writers portray Jesus Christ as both the son of God and the son of David.[1] Through his sacrificial death and triumphant resurrection, Jesus Christ redeems people from the power of evil and ransoms them from the domain of death, sanctifying them so that they may eventually come into the presence of God clothed in a righteousness derived from Christ.

Christ's death, resurrection, and ascension mark a new era in the history of the world, as God's kingdom is inaugurated, but a further period of time will pass before God intervenes decisively to destroy completely the powers of evil, before constructing his holy city, New Jerusalem, on a renewed earth.

Since the distinctive subject of this book is the city of God, this chapter will concentrate on various related ways in which the New Testament writings portray the development of God's plan to establish his temple-city on the earth. The first of these concerns the replacement of the Jerusalem temple by a new spiritual temple, the church. This transition means that the city of Jerusalem is no longer the sole location of God's presence on earth. Second, a negative portrayal of Jerusalem, especially in Matthew's Gospel, anticipates the destruction of the Jerusalem temple by the Romans in AD 70. This significant event brings to an end any possibility of Jerusalem continuing to be God's dwelling place on earth. Without a temple inhabited by the Lord, Jerusalem is no different from any other city. Third,

---

1. See Graeme Goldsworthy, *The Son of God and the New Creation*, Short Studies in Biblical Theology (Wheaton, IL: Crossway, 2015).

various New Testament passages focus on how Jesus's followers enjoy the privilege of being citizens of a heavenly city that will eventually become a worldwide cosmopolitan city upon a renewed earth. With the re-creation of heaven and earth, God and his redeemed people will live together in an extraordinary metropolis.

The Church as God's Spiritual Temple

The New Testament writings witness to the transformation of the Jerusalem temple into a new, spiritual temple that is created by those who are inhabited by the Holy Spirit. The followers of Jesus become the new earthly dwelling place of God.[2] This development has implications for how the temple-city of Jerusalem is perceived. For the early church, the temple in Jerusalem and its sacrificial system become redundant. No longer is the kingdom of God associated with a particular political entity, for the kingdom begins to spread throughout the world. As the book of Acts reveals, the movement is from Jerusalem outward to Rome. Wherever Christian communities are formed, God may be found dwelling in their midst through the Holy Spirit. No longer can Jerusalem claim to have the exclusive privilege of being God's unique temple-city, the sole earthly location of God's presence.

As the church becomes God's earthly residence, an important change occurs. In the Old Testament God lived *among* his people; in the New Testament he lives *within* them. As R. E. Clements helpfully observes:

> The ancient promises that God would dwell with his people were eagerly taken up by Christians and applied to the Church, the Body of Christ, in which God dwelt by the Holy Spirit. The major difference between the new fulfilment and

---

2. For a fuller discussion, see T. Desmond Alexander, *From Eden to the New Jerusalem: An Introduction to Biblical Theology* (Grand Rapids, MI: Kregel, 2009), 60–73.

the old promise is that whereas the Old Testament had spoken of a dwelling of God among men, the New Testament speaks of a dwelling of God within men by the Holy Spirit.[3]

The apostle Paul alludes to the church as God's dwelling place in his letter to the Ephesians. Writing to a mainly Gentile audience he says,

> So then you are no longer strangers and aliens, but you are fellow citizens with the saints and members of the household of God, built on the foundation of the apostles and prophets, Christ Jesus himself being the cornerstone, in whom the whole structure, being joined together, grows into a holy temple in the Lord. In him you also are being built together into a dwelling place for God by the Spirit. (Eph. 2:19–22)

For Paul, the corporate church is God's temple, with Jesus Christ being the cornerstone, the apostles and prophets being the foundation. Although God already dwells within this new temple, the whole edifice continues to grow.

Paul also writes about the church being the temple of God in his letter to the believers in Corinth. He remarks:

> Do you not know that you are God's temple and that God's Spirit dwells in you? If anyone destroys God's temple, God will destroy him. For God's temple is holy, and you are that temple. (1 Cor. 3:16–17).[4]

Paul later says, "Or do you not know that your body is a temple of the Holy Spirit within you, whom you have from God?" (1 Cor.

---

3. Ronald E. Clements, *God and Temple: The Idea of the Divine Presence in Ancient Israel* (Oxford, UK: Basil Blackwell, 1965), 139.

4. The Greek for "you" is plural in vv. 16 and 17.

6:19).[5] In a subsequent letter Paul writes, "What agreement has the temple of God with idols? For we are the temple of the living God; as God said, 'I will make my dwelling among them and walk among them, and I will be their God, and they shall be my people'" (2 Cor. 6:16). In all of these passages, Paul addresses all of the church members as a corporate body. Together they form God's dwelling place. Consequently, as Paul contends, they must live holy lives.

The apostle Peter also considers the church to be God's temple. In 1 Peter 2:4–8 Peter quotes from three Old Testament passages: Isaiah 28:16; Psalm 118:22; and Isaiah 8:14. The use of these passages recalls Peter's message to Jewish leaders in Jerusalem in Acts 4. He tells them, "This Jesus is the stone that was rejected by you, the builders, which has become the cornerstone. And there is salvation in no one else, for there is no other name under heaven given among men by which we must be saved" (Acts 4:1–12; cf. Matt. 21:42; Mark 12:10; Luke 20:17). According to Thomas, New Testament texts like 1 Peter 2:6 "draw upon the Zion imagery of Isaiah 28:16 // Ps 118:22 to reinforce the foundation for the church is none other than Christ. So 'Zion' refers to the people of God constructed upon the Christ, Zion's cornerstone."[6] As the new temple of God, the church takes its shape from Jesus Christ, the cornerstone.

The transition of God's earthly residence from the Jerusalem temple to the church may be associated with the coming of the Spirit at Pentecost, as described in Acts 2. The description of this event parallels closely the accounts of God's presence filling the tabernacle (Ex. 40:34–35) and the temple (1 Kings 8:10–11; 2 Chron. 7:1–2).[7]

---

5. "You" and "your" are plural in this verse. Paul is speaking here not of the bodies of individual believers but of the corporate body of the church.

6. H. A. Thomas, "Zion," in *Dictionary of the Old Testament: Prophets*, ed. M. J. Boda and J. G. McConville (Downers Grove, IL: IVP Academic, 2012), 913.

7. Cf. G. K. Beale, *The Temple and the Church's Mission: A Biblical Theology of the Dwelling Place of God*, New Studies in Biblical Theology 17 (Leicester, UK: Apollos, 2004), 201–16; Beale, "Eden, the Temple, and the Church's Mission in the New Creation," *JETS* 48 (2005): 64–66.

The Jerusalem experience is then followed by two similar events: the first involves the coming of the Spirit upon Samaritans (Acts 8:14–17); the next involves the Spirit coming upon Gentiles at the house of Cornelius (Acts 10:44–47). These parallel events, which involve people from different nations being incorporated into God's new temple, signal a movement away from God's residence being linked solely to Jerusalem.

Since the church or kingdom of God/heaven is not defined by geographical location, the concept of a physical, holy temple-city becomes a future hope rather than a present reality. Consequently, New Testament authors do not look for the reinstatement of Jerusalem as a temple-city prior to the return of Jesus Christ and the renewing of the earth. To do so would run counter to their belief that through the Holy Spirit the church has become God's dwelling place on earth.

Jesus and Jerusalem

The Gospel according to Matthew, which is usually considered to be the most Jewish of the four canonical Gospels, reflects a movement away from Jerusalem as the city of God in a number of ways.[8] In Matthew's Gospel Jesus is associated more strongly with Galilee than Jerusalem. Jesus begins and ends his ministry in Galilee, in fulfillment of Isaiah 9:1–2:

> Now when he heard that John had been arrested, he withdrew into Galilee. And leaving Nazareth he went and lived in Capernaum by the sea, in the territory of Zebulun and Naphtali, so that what was spoken by the prophet Isaiah might be fulfilled: "The land of Zebulun and the land of Naphtali, the

---

8. For a fuller discussion of Jerusalem in Matthew and the other Gospels, see L. K. Fuller Dow, *Images of Zion: Biblical Antecedents for the New Jerusalem*, New Testament Monographs 26 (Sheffield, UK: Sheffield Phoenix Press, 2010), 140–65.

way of the sea, beyond the Jordan, Galilee of the Gentiles—
the people dwelling in darkness have seen a great light, and
for those dwelling in the region and shadow of death, on them
a light has dawned." (Matt. 4:12–16)

Of significance is the fact that Galilee is described here as "Galilee
of the Gentiles" or perhaps more accurately "Galilee of the nations"
(who are not Jews). Not only does Jesus begin his ministry in Galilee,
but it is in Galilee that he gives his final commission to the disciples
after his resurrection. In doing so, he sends them out into the world
to make disciples of all nations.

Strangely perhaps, in Matthew's Gospel Jerusalem is portrayed
as the center of power for those who oppose Jesus. Jesus is not born
in Jerusalem, but King Herod lives there (Matt. 2:1–3). The Jewish
authorities, who claim authority over the temple but seek the death of
Jesus, are located in Jerusalem. This negative portrayal of Jerusalem
is highlighted in the way Jesus speaks of his own death occurring in
Jerusalem:

> From that time Jesus began to show his disciples that he must
> go to Jerusalem and suffer many things from the elders and
> chief priests and scribes, and be killed, and on the third day
> be raised. (Matt. 16:21)

> And as Jesus was going up to Jerusalem, he took the twelve
> disciples aside, and on the way he said to them, "See, we are
> going up to Jerusalem. And the Son of Man will be delivered
> over to the chief priests and scribes, and they will condemn
> him to death." (Matt. 20:17–18)

Jesus laments over Jerusalem with words that underline the waywardness of the city:

> O Jerusalem, Jerusalem, the city that kills the prophets and stones those who are sent to it! How often would I have gathered your children together as a hen gathers her brood under her wings, and you were not willing! (Matt. 23:37)

Far from being the "city of God," Jerusalem is presented as opposing God. In light of this, Jesus predicts in Matthew 24 the destruction of the temple.[9] When it is later destroyed by the Romans in AD 70, this event confirms that God no longer dwells in Jerusalem. Jerusalem post AD 70 cannot claim to be the temple-city where God dwells.

The emphasis given to Galilee in Matthew's Gospel symbolizes a transformation brought about by Jesus Christ. This is reflected in what Jesus has to say at the start of the Sermon on the Mount. On a mountain location Jesus mentions various characteristics that mark those who shall be blessed by God:

> Blessed are the poor in spirit, for theirs is the kingdom of heaven. Blessed are those who mourn, for they shall be comforted. Blessed are the meek, for they shall inherit the earth. Blessed are those who hunger and thirst for righteousness, for they shall be satisfied. Blessed are the merciful, for they shall receive mercy. Blessed are the pure in heart, for they shall see God. Blessed are the peacemakers, for they shall be called sons of God. Blessed are those who are persecuted for righteousness' sake, for theirs is the kingdom of heaven. Blessed are you when others revile you and persecute you and utter all kinds of evil against you falsely on my account. Rejoice and be glad, for your reward is great in heaven, for

---

9. The book of Malachi reveals that even in the postexilic period the temple was defiled by those who served and worshiped there. Christ's remarks about Jerusalem in Matt. 23:37 and Luke 13:34 convey something of God's frustration at the city's response to its privileged status.

so they persecuted the prophets who were before you. (Matt. 5:3–12)

All the qualities listed by Jesus are associated in the Old Testament with ascending the holy mountain in order to live in the presence of God. Most striking are the references to inheriting the earth and seeing God.[10] Everything promised in verses 4–8 concerns the future; only verses 3 and 10 have promises that relate to the present. Moreover, verses 11–12 imply that for the present there will be ongoing hostility in this world for Jesus's followers from those opposed to God. The hope expressed in the Beatitudes resembles the eschatological hope of the Old Testament prophets (cf. Isa. 61:1–3).

In the Gospels the kingdom of God/heaven is not defined by geographical borders. At this time, as for preceding centuries, Jerusalem was under the control of Gentile nations. Although many Jews expected the Messiah to usher in a period of political independence, the coming of Jesus as Messiah does not bring this about. The divine construction of New Jerusalem on a re-created earth will be fulfilled only when Christ returns.

Citizens of a Heavenly City

The concept of a divinely constructed city figures prominently within Hebrews 11 in a passage that recalls the faith of the patriarchs of Genesis. According to the author of Hebrews, Abraham's faith is reflected in the fact that he looked forward to "a better country," a "heavenly one," "the city that has foundations, whose designer and builder is God" (Heb. 11:8–16). Particular emphasis is given to Abraham's anticipation of this future city. The author of Hebrews stresses

---

10. On inheriting the earth, see Oren R. Martin, *Bound for the Promised Land: The Land Promise in God's Redemptive Plan*, New Studies in Biblical Theology 34 (Downers Grove, IL: InterVarsity Press, 2015), 124–26.

that Abraham's journey to a foreign land was motivated by his "looking forward" to this God-created metropolis.[11]

However, Abraham, Isaac, and Jacob did not receive the promised city during their lifetime on earth; they merely saw it and greeted it from afar. They did not see it in the present, but they hoped for it in the future. As the author of Hebrews rightly concludes, the patriarchs anticipated this city by faith, for as the opening verse of Hebrews 11 states, "Now faith is the assurance of things hoped for, the conviction of things not seen" (v. 1).

Hebrews 11 presents the patriarchs as looking forward toward a city that will be inhabited beyond this present life. Referring to Abraham and those who lived by faith, he writes:

> And all these, though commended through their faith, did not receive what was promised, since God had provided something better for us, that apart from us they should not be made perfect. (Heb. 11:39–40)

In saying this, the author of Hebrews expects that both he and his readers will join all those previously mentioned in chapter 11, including Abraham, Isaac, and Jacob, in receiving what was promised. When this happens, they will be made perfect, "arriving at the goal of God's saving purposes."[12]

The author of Hebrews links the future experience of all believers to a city. In chapter 12 he refers once more to this city, describing it as "the city of the living God, the heavenly Jerusalem" (v. 22). He then makes one further reference to this city, noting that "here we have no lasting city, but we seek the city that is to come" (Heb. 13:14).

The author of Hebrews says little about the nature of this "city

---

11. To understand the Hebrew reading, the call of Abraham in Gen. 12:1–3 has to be read against the background of Genesis 1–11, and especially the building of Babel-Babylon in Gen. 11:1–9.

12. Donald A. Hagner, *Hebrews*, NIBCNT (Peabody, MA: Hendrickson, 1983), 210.

that is to come," but a fuller picture is provided in the vision that the apostle John describes in Revelation 21–22. John sees "the holy city, new Jerusalem, coming down out of heaven from God, prepared as a bride adorned for her husband" (Rev. 21:2).[13] He goes on to describe the city's enormous size and splendor. This is no common city, for it fills the entire earth and is constructed largely of gold. For John, this unique metropolis is the goal toward which creation is moving, bringing to fulfillment the process that God initiated in Genesis 1.

Since John sees this city in a vision, we ought to interpret with caution what is recorded. Aspects of John's visions in Revelation are symbolic in nature. For example, in figurative language, Jesus is often designated as a lamb (e.g., Rev. 5:6, 8, 12–13; 6:1, 16). Because John's visions contain symbolic images, everything that John says about the city need not be taken literally. Nevertheless, one senses that John's vision of the new Jerusalem foretells the future existence of a real city on a real, but renewed, earth.

The city in John's vision is far from ordinary. He records:

> The one who spoke with me had a measuring rod of gold to measure the city and its gates and walls. The city lies four-square, its length the same as its width. And he measured the city with his rod, 12,000 stadia. Its length and width and height are equal. He also measured its wall, 144 cubits by human measurement, which is also an angel's measurement. The wall was built of jasper, while the city was pure gold, like clear glass. (Rev. 21:15–18)

---

13. John subsequently records, "And he carried me away in the Spirit to a great, high mountain, and showed me the holy city Jerusalem coming down out of heaven from God" (Rev. 21:10), repeating the ideas of the holy city coming down from heaven. John also writes of seeing "a new heaven and a new earth" (Rev. 21:1). The association of the new heaven and new earth with New Jerusalem recalls Isa. 65:17–18.

The actual dimensions may be symbolic, as is often the case in this type of literature, but they nevertheless convey something of the city's enormous size. In terms of length, breadth, and height, each side is 12,000 stadia (that is, 1,380 miles or 2,220 kilometers). While the exceptional size of the city is amazing, even by modern standards, its shape is even more peculiar; it is a perfect cube.

As many commentators observe, the proportions of the city match those of the Most Holy Place in the Jerusalem temple constructed by Solomon: "The inner sanctuary was twenty cubits long, twenty cubits wide, and twenty cubits high" (1 Kings 6:20). New Jerusalem and the Most Holy Place are the only perfect cubes mentioned in the Bible. And both are made of gold. While the inner sanctuary of the Jerusalem temple was overlaid with gold (1 Kings 6:20), Revelation 21:18 records that "the city was pure gold." Since God's presence is associated with both structures, John's vision implies that the new Jerusalem in its entirety is an enlarged Most Holy Place. For this reason, John sees no temple building within the new Jerusalem: "I saw no temple in the city, for its temple is the Lord God the Almighty and the Lamb" (Rev. 21:22). The whole city is a sanctuary, where God is served and worshiped by every citizen. This implies that everyone living in the city has a priestly status (cf. Rev. 22:4). This vision of ultimate reality takes on added significance when we consider how the whole biblical story, beginning in Genesis, is constructed around the idea of the earth becoming God's dwelling place.

Various details within John's vision suggest that New Jerusalem is an expanded garden of Eden. Within the city stands the "tree of life," to which people have easy access:

> Then the angel showed me the river of the water of life, bright as crystal, flowing from the throne of God and of the Lamb through the middle of the street of the city; also, on either

side of the river, the tree of life with its twelve kinds of fruit,
yielding its fruit each month. The leaves of the tree were for
the healing of the nations. (Rev. 22:1–2)

Remarkably, this life-enhancing tree functions for the benefit of the
nations, implying that New Jerusalem is the ultimate cosmopolitan
city (cf. Rev. 21:24–26). New Jerusalem is inhabited by people from
many nations. As co-dwellers with God, the people experience his
presence in such an intimate way that they see his face. No barrier
stands between God and those who dwell in the city. This intimacy
is almost unique in the whole of the Bible, recalling how Adam and
Eve knew God prior to their expulsion from the garden of Eden.

New Jerusalem is portrayed as a utopia, a paradise. As John notes,
all evil and suffering is banished from this metropolis. As a holy
city under the absolute control of a perfect deity, the new Jerusalem
provides a perfect environment for its inhabitants. The city cannot
change for the better because it is already perfect, and being perfect
it cannot change for the worse.

In Revelation New Jerusalem is contrasted with another city. The
book of Revelation provides visions of not one city, but two. John's
vision of New Jerusalem in 21:9–22:9 stands alongside the vision of
another city that is very different, a city symbolically named Babylon
(Rev. 14:8; 16:19; 17:5; 18:2, 10, 21).

Whereas God will build New Jerusalem in the future, the city of
Babylon already exists. Present here and now, Babylon is the great
human city constructed by people who arrogantly and boldly defy
God. Babylon and New Jerusalem represent contrasting worlds, a
fact reflected in their distinctive locations. Babylon is placed in
the wilderness (Rev. 17:3), but New Jerusalem is on a mountaintop
(Rev. 21:10).

As we move between the wilderness and the great, high

mountain, the visions of the two cities abound in fascinating contrasts. Both are pictured as women. New Jerusalem is "the Bride, the wife of the Lamb" (Rev. 21:9; cf. Rev. 19:6–8), but Babylon is the "great prostitute" (Rev. 17:1–5). As a prostitute, Babylon deceives and manipulates the "peoples and multitudes and nations and languages" with her alluring charm (Rev. 17:15). She makes the nations drunk with wine, as well as enticing them to engage in sexual immorality. These activities are combined to accentuate the truly evil nature of Babylon. Babylon represents those who have deserted God and replaced him with other lovers.

As a prostitute, Babylon has prospered. She is dressed in expensive clothes, "adorned with gold and jewels and pearls" (Rev. 17:4), and she holds a golden cup in her hand. Babylon's wealth features frequently throughout Revelation 18. The city abounds with excessive riches due to an obsession with acquiring luxurious goods. Her entrepreneurs are "the great ones of the earth" (Rev. 18:23). Consequently, with the city's destruction, "the merchants of the earth weep and mourn" (Rev. 18:11), for there no longer exists a market for their "cargo of gold, silver, jewels, pearls, fine linen, purple cloth, silk, scarlet cloth, all kinds of scented wood, all kinds of articles of ivory, all kinds of articles of costly wood, bronze, iron and marble, cinnamon, spice, incense, myrrh, frankincense, wine, oil, fine flour, wheat, cattle and sheep, horses and chariots, and slaves, that is, human souls" (Rev. 18:12–13). Shipmasters and sailors will also mourn over the city's destruction (Rev. 18:17–19), for with Babylon's demise there will no longer be any trade for them.

This picture of Babylon reveals how humanity's obsession with wealth and power becomes a substitute for knowing God. History confirms the ongoing existence of "Babylon,"[14] as economics domi-

---

14. The Babylon of Revelation is often taken to be a cipher for Rome, the greatest "city" in the first century AD. However, we should not restrict the interpretation of Babylon to merely the capital of the Roman Empire. Babylon symbolizes what humans strive after when separated from God and is the antithesis of the city that God himself wishes to build on the earth.

nates national and international politics, with nations using their power to grow rich at the expense of others.

Unlike the opulent prostitute Babylon with her glittering jewelry (Rev. 17:4), New Jerusalem is portrayed as a bride, dressed in a linen dress—presumably white—that speaks of purity (Rev. 19:8). By placing side by side the visions of the prostitute, that is Babylon, and the bride of the Lamb, that is New Jerusalem, John vividly contrasts the faithlessness of the former with the faithfulness of the latter. True love will be found only in God's presence; what the prostitute offers is but a fleeting, deceitful shadow of the real thing.

New Jerusalem offers wholeness and love in the presence of God. Since this inheritance lies in the future, the citizens of New Jerusalem must live as exiles or pilgrims for the present in Babylon. In this sense the "Babylonian exile" is still ongoing. While Jesus Christ's first coming inaugurates a new age, this overlaps with the old age. The divine re-creation of the earth and the coming of New Jerusalem awaits the return of Jesus Christ. Fittingly, the book of Revelation presents an important choice to its readers. Will they live as citizens of this world's godless Babylon or as citizens of God's future New Jerusalem? To those who remain faithful, Jesus promises the privilege of reigning with him (Rev. 3:21).

The Hope of Bodily Resurrection

The New Testament idea of a future New Jerusalem is very much in keeping with the emphasis that is placed upon the hope of bodily resurrection linked to the return of Jesus Christ (cf. Heb. 11:39–40). We see this reflected most fully in the teachings of the apostle Paul.

Paul had a strong belief that this present life is only part of something much greater. One reason for this was Paul's conviction that death is not the end of human existence. Focusing especially on the resurrection of Jesus Christ, Paul believed that the followers of Jesus will also experience a similar resurrection (1 Cor. 15:12–28). In Philippians 3:11 Paul refers specifically to his hope of attaining "the resurrection from the dead."

From his letters, Paul conveys three important ideas about the resurrection of Jesus's followers, which have implications for understanding the concept of New Jerusalem. First, Paul believes that those who trust in Jesus Christ for salvation experience in this life a spiritual resurrection. Second, he is strongly convinced of a future bodily or physical resurrection for those who physically die in Christ. Third, he associates the bodily resurrection of believers with a future return of Jesus Christ.

In Paul's thinking the new age begins with Jesus Christ's own resurrection. As Costa notes,

> The coming of Jesus, his death but especially his resurrection inaugurated the ushering in of the eschaton. . . . Paul believed that the end of the ages had arrived (. . . 1 Cor. 10:11), and the starting point of the "ends of the ages" seems to be the resurrection of Jesus, who is now the "firstfruits" from the dead (1 Cor 15:20).[15]

Paul undoubtedly sees himself as living in the new age, but he recognizes that this new age will be fully consummated only with the return of Jesus Christ. To describe this situation, some scholars speak of "realized eschatology" and "future eschatology," two categories that are sometimes labeled "already" and "not yet":

> For Paul, believers live between two crucial moments: the resurrection and the parousia of Jesus. As a result salvation has an "already" and a "not yet" component. Because of the res-

15. Tony Costa, "'Is Saul of Tarsus Also among the Prophets?' Paul's Calling as Prophetic Divine Commissioning," in *Christian Origins and Greco-Roman Culture: Social and Literary Contexts for the New Testament*, ed. S. E. Porter and A. W. Pitts (Leiden: Brill, 2012), 209.

urrection [of Jesus], Christ-believers are already united with Jesus, sealed with the Spirit, forgiven of their sins and more than conquerors. On the other hand, salvation is not yet complete because sin and death are still active, though wounded, adversaries. Until the parousia they remain under constant threats. But when Christ returns, the dead are raised, the living are transformed and sin along with death is destroyed.[16]

Paul's understanding of how the resurrection of Jesus Christ inaugurates a "new age" is consistent with his belief that the followers of Jesus become citizens of the heavenly Jerusalem. In Galatians 4:21–31 Paul contrasts the "present Jerusalem," which he associates with slavery to the law, with the "Jerusalem above," which brings freedom. In Philippians 3:20 he remarks, "Our citizenship is in heaven, and from it we await a Savior, the Lord Jesus Christ." While Jesus's followers have the privilege of citizenship of the heavenly Jerusalem, they must await the return of Jesus before this city is established on a renewed earth, bringing to fulfillment God's purpose in creating this world. The whole of history is moving toward a great, unending climax.

Regarding Paul's understanding of a future bodily resurrection, it is important to observe that Paul does not consider the ultimate afterlife experience to be a form of life in which the soul exists apart from a body. However, he affirms that the resurrection body will be far superior to the pre-resurrection body. To illustrate this Paul uses the example of a seed that is sown in the ground. He writes in 1 Corinthians 15:35–44:

> But someone will ask, "How are the dead raised? With what kind of body do they come?" You foolish person! What you

---

16. David B. Capes, Rodney Reeves, and E. Randolph Richards, *Rediscovering Paul: An Introduction to His World, Letters and Theology* (Nottingham, UK: Apollos, 2007), 261.

> sow does not come to life unless it dies. And what you sow is
> not the body that is to be, but a bare kernel, perhaps of wheat
> or of some other grain. But God gives it a body as he has
> chosen, and to each kind of seed its own body. . . . So is it with
> the resurrection of the dead. What is sown is perishable; what
> is raised is imperishable. It is sown in dishonor; it is raised in
> glory. It is sown in weakness; it is raised in power. It is sown a
> natural body; it is raised a spiritual body. If there is a natural
> body, there is also a spiritual body. (1 Cor. 15:35–44)

Although Paul speaks in verse 44 of a "spiritual body," he does not
mean a noncorporeal body. According to Thiselton, Paul's "spiritual
body . . . implies a self which is recognizable and identifiable publicly,
but animated and characterized by the Holy Spirit."[17] Thiselton goes
on to say: "Paul is addressing the problem of moral transformation
as the raised Christian enters God's immediate presence, rather than
a change into a non-material mode of existence."[18]

Paul also associates the resurrection of believers with a future
return of Jesus Christ. To understand Paul's thinking about this, it
is helpful to observe that in his time Jewish thinking about history
involved the idea of two ages. There was the present evil age and a
coming new age. The present evil age was characterized by a world
in which God's authority was largely rejected by people. This will
ultimately be replaced by a new age when God will intervene significantly to overthrow all that is evil. In Jewish expectation, the transition from the present evil age to the coming new age was closely
associated with the restoration of the Davidic monarchy, involving a
God-sent messiah. For Paul, Jesus was this Messiah or Christ. In the
opening words of Paul's epistle to the Romans, he writes:

---

17. Anthony C. Thiselton, *The Living Paul: An Introduction to the Apostle and His Thought*
(London: SPCK, 2009), 72.
18. Ibid.

Paul, a servant of Christ Jesus, called to be an apostle, set apart for the gospel of God, which he promised beforehand through his prophets in the holy Scriptures, concerning his Son, who was descended from David according to the flesh and was declared to be the Son of God in power according to the Spirit of holiness by his resurrection from the dead, Jesus Christ our Lord, through whom we have received grace and apostleship to bring about the obedience of faith for the sake of his name among all the nations, including you who are called to belong to Jesus Christ, To all those in Rome who are loved by God and called to be saints: Grace to you and peace from God our Father and the Lord Jesus Christ. (Rom. 1:1–7)

In this passage Paul draws attention to Jesus being descended from David, but he also highlights here that Jesus has been resurrected from death. For Paul, the resurrection of Jesus Christ anticipates and makes possible the resurrection of others. In writing to the church at Corinth, Paul comments:

But in fact Christ has been raised from the dead, the first-fruits of those who have fallen asleep. For as by a man came death, by a man has come also the resurrection of the dead. For as in Adam all die, so also in Christ shall all be made alive. But each in his own order: Christ the firstfruits, then at his coming those who belong to Christ. Then comes the end, when he delivers the kingdom to God the Father after destroying every rule and every authority and power. For he must reign until he has put all his enemies under his feet. (1 Cor. 15:20–25)

Paul speaks here of Jesus being the "firstfruits of those who have fallen asleep" (v. 20). He then associates the resurrection of others with Christ's coming (v. 23) and finally speaks of the end (v. 24). Although Paul understands the resurrection of Jesus to have already taken place, he looks to the future coming of Jesus Christ as being the time when a general bodily resurrection of the dead will take place.

When he refers to the coming of Jesus, Paul uses the Greek term *parousia*. This term is sometimes used in the New Testament to refer to ordinary people "coming" to visit someone (e.g., 1 Cor. 16:17). However, it is also used in the Gospels to refer to the "coming of the Son of Man" (Matt. 24:27, 37, 39). In what may be one of the earliest known letters of Paul, he describes the coming of Jesus in this way to the believers in Thessalonica:

> But we do not want you to be uninformed, brothers, about those who are asleep, that you may not grieve as others do who have no hope. For since we believe that Jesus died and rose again, even so, through Jesus, God will bring with him those who have fallen asleep. For this we declare to you by a word from the Lord, that we who are alive, who are left until the coming of the Lord, will not precede those who have fallen asleep. For the Lord himself will descend from heaven with a cry of command, with the voice of an archangel, and with the sound of the trumpet of God. And the dead in Christ will rise first. Then we who are alive, who are left, will be caught up together with them in the clouds to meet the Lord in the air, and so we will always be with the Lord. Therefore encourage one another with these words. (1 Thess. 4:13–18)

Here Paul associates the resurrection of the dead with the coming of Jesus Christ.

Paul's description of the future coming of Jesus Christ may well be influenced by how the Greek term *parousia* was understood in the first century when referring to an imperial visit. Such visits were undertaken with pomp and ceremony. This would explain Paul's reference to the archangel's voice and the sound of God's trumpet, which announce the arrival of the one who is coming.

Alongside the term *parousia*, Paul introduces the expression *eis apantēsin*, which means "to meet." According to Gene Green, "*To meet (eis apantēsin) was almost a technical term that described the custom of sending a delegation outside the city to receive a dignitary who was on the way to town.*"[19] This practice is described in Acts 28:15, where the expression *eis apantēsin* is also used: "The brothers there [in Rome], when they heard about us [Paul and others], came as far as the Forum of Appius and Three Taverns to meet us. On seeing them, Paul thanked God and took courage." After the meeting outside of the city, the dignitary was escorted in a grand procession into the city.

If we apply this ancient practice to Paul's description in 1 Thessalonians 4, the following picture emerges. Paul wants to reassure the Thessalonians that those who are already dead shall be the first to arise to meet the coming king. Although they are dead, they shall not be disadvantaged when Christ returns. Those who are resurrected shall then be joined by those who are alive, and together they shall all meet Jesus Christ as he returns to the earth. Moreover, Paul pictures all of these people escorting Jesus to earth. Paul does not think of them as flying off to heaven. Unfortunately, this passage is often misunderstood as implying that the followers of Jesus shall be removed from the earth in an event that is commonly called "the rapture."

Conclusion

Drawing on the testimony of the New Testament, it is evident that the early church saw in the death, resurrection, and ascension of

---

19. Gene L. Green, *The Letters to the Thessalonians*, PNTC (Grand Rapids, MI: Eerdmans, 2002), 226.

Jesus Christ the beginning of a new era in God's activity in the world. Among the various features that witness to this, the following are noteworthy, as we have observed in this chapter. First, the church becomes the new temple of God, making obsolete the Jerusalem temple. Second, the negative portrayal of Jerusalem in the Gospels implies that it can no longer be considered to be God's "holy city." Third, the early church anticipated the future creation of a new city of God that would replace the wicked "Babylon" of the present. The followers of Jesus were to consider themselves citizens of this "heavenly city." Fourth, the bodily resurrection of Jesus's followers at his return was a necessary development in order for them to live within the New Jerusalem.

Although Jesus in his teaching makes no direct reference to New Jerusalem, he clearly envisages a future in which his followers will inherit the earth and enjoy the privilege of seeing God (Matt. 5:5, 8). This expectation is reflected in his words of reassurance to his disciples:

> Let not your hearts be troubled. Believe in God; believe also in me. In my Father's house are many rooms. If it were not so, would I have told you that I go to prepare a place for you? And if I go and prepare a place for you, I will come again and will take you to myself, that where I am you may be also. (John 14:1–3)

8

Anticipating New Jerusalem

The preceding chapters have explored how the concept of a unique city occupies a central place within the biblical story. God's purpose in creating this world is to establish a resplendent metropolis that will fill the earth, where God will reside in harmony with humans. Progress toward the construction of this city, however, is not straightforward.

Although God delegates authority to Adam and Eve to begin the process of establishing his divine kingdom on the earth, they succumb to the temptation of the cunning Serpent. Consequently, humanity is alienated from God, and the earth comes under the control of the Evil One. People are, however, innately city builders, and so they arrogantly proceed to build cities for themselves, without acknowledging any dependence upon their Creator. While they have the capacity to achieve much, the perversity of human nature mars all that they do. Their best efforts come at a cost, as autonomous people struggle with each other for supremacy. Focused on founding their own empires, they fill the earth with violence directed toward other people and other creatures.

Against this background, the biblical story recounts how God takes the initiative to redeem people from the grip of the Evil One, gradually establishing his kingdom on the earth, not through violence but through sacrificial love. The Old Testament story of Israel's redemption from slavery in Egypt begins a process that climaxes with God coming to dwell on Mount Zion. This process provides a paradigm for understanding divine salvation, as God takes the initiative to create a holy temple-city. The events that lead to the construction of the temple in Jerusalem illustrate something of what salvation entails and how it is achieved. These events also anticipate a greater salvation that will come through a future Davidic king.

Becoming a Citizen of New Jerusalem

Adopting a typological reading of the Old Testament exodus-Sinai narrative, the apostle John interprets the crucifixion of Jesus as a Passover sacrifice (John 19:36). Jesus's death gives eternal life to those who believe in him. Born of the Spirit, believers are adopted as God's children, becoming members of the kingdom of God. They also enjoy the privilege of becoming citizens of New Jerusalem, although they must await the return of Jesus Christ before this city is established on a new earth.

Jesus's sacrificial death redeems his followers from the power of evil, ransoms them from the domain of death, cleanses them from defilement, and makes them holy. All these steps are necessary before sinful people may dwell in God's holy presence. This is all of grace, God's gift freely offered to those who willingly turn from their sin.

Living in Babylon

By believing in the concept of a future holy city, New Jerusalem, Christians run the risk of being ridiculed for promoting a "pie in the sky when you die" mentality. Yet such an outlook does not reflect the teaching of the Bible. Jesus did not teach his disciples to pray, "Take me to heaven," but rather, "Your kingdom come, your will be done, on earth as it is in heaven" (Matt. 6:10).

For those who are united to Jesus Christ, eternal life begins here and now, as does citizenship of the city that will one day be created by God on a renewed earth. Jesus challenges his followers to look forward in faith, to pray and work for the spread of God's rule here and now. They are to exercise true humility, remembering that they have been redeemed from evil only by the grace of God and not by their own achievements or piety. They are to witness to an alternative worldview that promotes belief in a Creator God, highlighting the inadequacy of a purely materialistic view of human existence. They are to be peacemakers, reconciling those who are alienated, especially from God. They are to make disciples of Jesus Christ, extending God's kingdom throughout the world through self-sacrificial love. They are to hunger and thirst after righteousness, caring for the oppressed and promoting social justice for the benefit of the marginalized. They are to resist the powers of evil, arming themselves for the spiritual battle that continues to rage until Christ returns. They are to consider themselves exiles and pilgrims in "Babylon," holding lightly to this life but living in this absurd and evil world in confident anticipation of all that God will yet do. They are to live holy lives, aiming for personal moral perfection and purity. They are to love others wholeheartedly, including their enemies, as an expression and outworking of their sincere love for God. They are to fulfill their creative capacity as home and city builders but ever recognizing the temporary nature of this present world.

Jesus Christ calls his followers to be kingdom builders here and now, but they are to do this with the confident assurance that Christ will return to address every injustice as universal judge, vindicating and punishing as appropriate. Only then with the defeat of evil will God establish New Jerusalem on a renewed earth.

The Christian's Ultimate Hope

The eighteenth-century evangelical Anglican minister John Newton, slave trader turned abolitionist after his remarkable conversion, is well known as the composer of the hymn "Amazing Grace." Outstanding among his other compositions is the hymn "Glorious Things of Thee Are Spoken, Zion, City of Our God." In five short stanzas he summarizes the essence of the biblical theology of New Jerusalem. Drawing inspiration from both Testaments, Newton passionately describes the benefits of being a citizen of New Jerusalem, before confidently proclaiming, "Solid joys and lasting treasure none but Zion's children know." This praise of Zion provides a fitting climax on which to conclude this study.

> Glorious things of thee are spoken,
> Zion, city of our God;
> He whose word cannot be broken
> Formed thee for His own abode.
> On the Rock of Ages founded,
> What can shake thy sure repose?
> With salvation's walls surrounded
> Thou may'st smile at all thy foes.
>
> See, the streams of living waters
> Springing from eternal love
> Well supply thy sons and daughters
> And all fear of want remove.
> Who can faint while such a river
> Ever flows their thirst t'assuage
> Grace, which, like the Lord, the Giver,
> Never fails from age to age?
>
> Round each habitation hovering,
> See the cloud and fire appear,

For a glory and a covering,
Showing that the Lord is near.
Thus they march, the pillar leading,
Light by night and shade by day,
Daily on the manna feeding
Which He gives them when they pray.

Blest inhabitants of Zion,
Washed in the Redeemer's blood!
Jesus, whom their souls rely on,
Makes them kings and priests to God.
'Tis His love His people raises
Over self to reign as kings,
And as priests, His solemn praises
Each for a thank-offering brings.

Savior, if of Zion's city
I through grace a member am,
Let the world deride or pity,
I will glory in Thy name.
Fading is the worldling's pleasure,
All his boasted pomp and show;
Solid joys and lasting treasure
None but Zion's children know.

For Further Reading

Alexander, T. Desmond. *Discovering Jesus: Four Gospels, One Person.* Nottingham, UK: Inter-Varsity Press, 2010.

———. *Exodus.* Apollos Old Testament Commentary. London: Apollos, 2017.

———. *Exodus.* Teach the Text. Grand Rapids, MI: Baker, 2016.

———. *From Eden to the New Jerusalem: An Introduction to Biblical Theology.* Grand Rapids, MI: Kregel, 2009.

———. *From Paradise to the Promised Land: An Introduction to the Pentateuch.* Grand Rapids, MI: Baker, 2012.

———. "Further Observations of the Term 'Seed' in Genesis." *Tyndale Bulletin* 48 (1997): 363–67.

———. "The Passover Sacrifice." In *Sacrifice in the Bible*, edited by R. T. Beckwith and M. Selman, 1–24. Grand Rapids, MI: Baker, 1995.

———. "The Regal Dimension of the תלדות־יעקב: Recovering the Literary Context of Genesis 37–50." In *Reading the Law: Studies in Honour of Gordon J. Wenham*, edited by J. G. McConville and K. Möller, 196–212. Library of Hebrew Bible/Old Testament Studies. Edinburgh: T&T Clark, 2007.

Anonymous. "Babel, Tower of." In *Dictionary of Biblical Imagery*, edited by L. Ryken, et al., 66–67. Downers Grove, IL: InterVarsity Press, 1998.

Arnold, Bill T. "Babylon." In *Dictionary of the Old Testament: Prophets*, edited by M. J. Boda and J. G. McConville, 53–60. Downers Grove, IL: IVP Academic, 2012.

Averbeck, Richard E. "Tabernacle." In *Dictionary of the Old Testament: Pentateuch*, edited by T. D. Alexander and D. W. Baker, 807–27. Downers Grove: InterVarsity Press, 2003.

Beale, G. K. "Eden, the Temple, and the Church's Mission in the New Creation." *Journal of the Evangelical Theological Society* 48 (2005): 5–31.

———. *The Temple and the Church's Mission: A Biblical Theology of the Dwelling Place of God*. New Studies in Biblical Theology 17. Leicester, UK: Apollos, 2004.

Beale, G. K., and Mitchell Kim, *God Dwells among Us: Expanding Eden to the Ends of the Earth*. Downers Grove, IL: InterVarsity Press, 2014.

Begg, C. T. "Babylon in the Book of Isaiah." In *The Book of Isaiah*, edited by J. Vermeylen, 121–25. Leuven: Leuven University Press,1989.

Block, Daniel I. *The Book of Ezekiel: Chapters 25–48*. New International Commentary on the Old Testament. Grand Rapids, MI: Eerdmans, 1998.

———. "Eden: A Temple? A Reassessment of the Biblical Evidence." In *From Creation to New Creation: Biblical Theology and Exegesis*, edited by D. M. Gurtner and B. L. Gladd, 3–29. Peabody, MA: Hendrickson, 2013.

Capes, David B., Rodney Reeves, and E. Randolph Richards, *Rediscovering Paul: An Introduction to His World, Letters and Theology*. Nottingham, UK: Apollos, 2007.

Cassuto, Umberto. *Commentary on Genesis*. Jerusalem: Magnes Press, 1961–1964.

Childs, Brevard S. *The Book of Exodus: A Critical, Theological Commentary*. Old Testament Library. London: SCM, 1974.

Clements, Ronald E. "The Davidic Covenant in the Isaiah Tradition." In *Covenant as Context: Essays in Honour of E.W. Nicholson*, edited by A. D. H. Mayes and R. B. Salters, 39–69. New York: Oxford University Press, 2003.

———. *God and Temple: The Idea of the Divine Presence in Ancient Israel*. Oxford, UK: Basil Blackwell, 1965.

Clifford, Richard J. *The Cosmic Mountain in Canaan and the Old Testament*. Harvard Semitic Monographs 4. Cambridge, MA: Harvard University Press, 1972.

Costa, Tony. "'Is Saul of Tarsus Also among the Prophets?' Paul's Calling as Prophetic Divine Commissioning." In *Christian Origins and Greco-Roman Culture: Social and Literary Contexts for the New Testament*, edited by S. E. Porter and A. W. Pitts, 203–36. Leiden: Brill, 2012.

Creach, Jerome F. D. *The Destiny of the Righteous in the Psalms*. St. Louis, MO: Chalice Press, 2008.

Dumbrell, William J. *The End of the Beginning: Revelation 21–22 and the Old Testament*. Grand Rapids, MI: Baker, 1985.

———. "Genesis 2:1–17: A Foreshadowing of the New Creation." In *Biblical Theology: Retrospect and Prospect*, edited by S. J. Hafemann, 53–65. Downers Grove, IL: InterVarsity Press, 2002.

Fuller Dow, L. K. *Images of Zion: Biblical Antecedents for the New Jerusalem*. New Testament Monographs 26. Sheffield, UK: Sheffield Phoenix Press, 2010.

Goldingay, John. *The Theology of the Book of Isaiah*. Downers Grove, IL: InterVarsity Press, 2014.

Goldsworthy, Graeme. *The Son of God and the New Creation*. Short Studies in Biblical Theology. Wheaton, IL: Crossway, 2015.

Gowan, Donald E. *Eschatology in the Old Testament*. Philadelphia: Fortress Press, 1986.

Green, Gene L. *The Letters to the Thessalonians*. Pillar New Testament Commentary. Grand Rapids, MI: Eerdmans, 2002.

Groves, J. Alan. "Zion Traditions." In *Dictionary of the Old Testament: Historical Books*, edited by B. T. Arnold and H. G. M. Williamson, 1,019–25. Downers Grove, IL: InterVarsity Press, 2005.

Hagner, Donald A. *Hebrews*. New International Biblical Commentary on the New Testament. Peabody, MA: Hendrickson, 1983.

Hom, Mary Katherine. "'. . . A Mighty Hunter before YHWH': Genesis 10:9 and the Moral-Theological Evaluation of Nimrod." *Vetus Testamentum* 60 (2010): 63–68.

Hoppe, Leslie J. *The Holy City: Jerusalem in the Theology of the Old Testament*. Collegeville, MN: Liturgical Press, 2000.

Hugenberger, G. P. "The Servant of the Lord in the 'Servant Songs' of Isaiah." In *The Lord's Anointed: Interpretation of Old Testament Messianic Texts*, edited by P. E. Satterthwaite, et al., 105–40. Grand Rapids, MI: Baker, 1995.

Larsson, Göran. *Bound for Freedom: The Book of Exodus in Jewish and Christian Traditions*. Peabody, MA: Hendrickson, 1999.

Lundquist, John M. "What Is a Temple? A Preliminary Typology." In *The Quest for the Kingdom of God: Studies in Honor of George E. Mendenhall*, edited by H. B. Huffmon, et al., 105–19. Winona Lake, IN: Eisenbrauns, 1983.

Martin, Oren R. *Bound for the Promised Land: The Land Promise in God's Redemptive Plan*. New Studies in Biblical Theology 34. Downers Grove, IL: InterVarsity Press, 2015.

McConville, Gordon. "Jerusalem in the Old Testament." In *Jerusalem Past and Present in the Purposes of God*, edited by P. W. L. Walker, 21–51. Croydon, UK: Deo Gloria Trust, 1992.

Merrill, Eugene H. "The Book of Ruth: Narration and Shared Themes." *Bibliotheca Sacra* 142 (1986): 130–39.

Meyers, Carol L. *The Tabernacle Menorah: A Synthetic Study of a Symbol from the Biblical Cult*. American Schools of Oriental Research Dissertation Series. Missoula, MT: Scholars Press, 1976.

———. "Temple, Jerusalem." *Anchor Bible Dictionary*, edited by David Noel Freedman, 6:350–69. New Haven, CT: Yale University Press, 1992.

Ollenburger, B. C. *Zion, City of the Great King: A Theological Symbol of the Jerusalem Cult*. Journal for the Study of the Old Testament Supplement Series 41. Sheffield, UK: JSOT Press, 1987.

Peterson, E. H., ed. "Isaiah: Introduction." In *The Message: The Bible in Contemporary Language: Numbered Edition*, 912–13. Colorado Springs: NavPress, 2005.

Petterson, Anthony R. *Haggai, Zechariah, and Malachi*. Apollos Old Testament Commentary 25. Downers Grove, IL: InterVarsity Press, 2015.

Poulsen, Frederik. *Representing Zion: Judgement and Salvation in the Old Testament*. Copenhagen International Seminar London. New York: Routledge, 2015.

Sarna, Nahum M. *Exploring Exodus: The Origins of Biblical Israel*. New York: Schocken, 1996.

Schmitz, Philip C. "The Grammar of Resurrection in Isaiah 26:19a-c." *Journal of Biblical Literature* 122 (2003): 145–49.

Schultz, Richard L. "Isaiah, Book of." In *Dictionary for Theological Interpretation of the Bible*, edited by K. J. Vanhoozer, et al., 336–44. Grand Rapids, MI: Baker Academic, 2005.

Smith, Gary V. *Isaiah 1–39*. New American Commentary 15A. Nashville: B&H, 2007.

Smith, Mark S. *The Pilgrimage Pattern in Exodus*. Journal for the Study of the Old Testament Supplement Series 239. Sheffield, UK: Sheffield Academic Press, 1997.

Soza, J. R. "Jeremiah." In *New Dictionary of Biblical Theology*, edited by T. D. Alexander and B. S. Rosner, 223–27. Downers Grove, IL: InterVarsity Press, 2000.

Taylor, J. B. "The Temple in Ezekiel." In *Heaven on Earth: The Temple in Biblical Theology*, edited by T. D. Alexander and S. Gathercole, 59–70. Carlisle, UK: Paternoster, 2004.

Thiselton, Anthony C. *The Living Paul: An Introduction to the Apostle and His Thought*. London: SPCK, 2009.

Thomas, H. A. "Zion." In *Dictionary of the Old Testament: Prophets*, edited by M. J. Boda and J. G. McConville, 907–14. Downers Grove, IL: IVP Academic, 2012.

Webb, Barry G. *The Message of Isaiah: On Eagles' Wings*. The Bible Speaks Today. Leicester, UK: Inter-Varsity Press, 1996.

———. "Zion in Transformation: A Literary Approach to Isaiah." In *The Bible in Three Dimensions*, edited by D. J. A. Clines, et al., 65–84. Journal for the Study of the Old Testament Supplement Series 87. Sheffield, UK: JSOT Press, 1990.

Wenham, Gordon J. "Sanctuary Symbolism in the Garden of Eden Story." *Proceedings of the World Congress of Jewish Studies* 9 (1986): 19–25.

General Index

'ābad (Hebrew: to serve, till), 18
Abraham, 31–34, 69; as a blessing to
    all the families of the earth, 70;
    in the book of Hebrews, 149–50;
    call of, 32, 150n11; construction
    of an altar on Mount Moriah by,
    34; deliberate contrast of with
    the people of Babel/Babylon, 32;
    and the promise of multiple de-
    scendants, 33–34, 69; renaming
    of (from Abram to Abraham),
    31; as the spiritual father of
    many nations, 69; willingness of
    to sacrifice Isaac, 69
Absalom, 82
Acts, book of, 143
Adam and Eve: Adam's role in Eden,
    18; disobedience of, 21, 23, 25,
    28, 31, 83, 141, 163; the experi-
    ence of God's presence prior to
    their expulsion from Eden, 153;
    expulsion of from Eden, 17, 22;
    as God's vice-regents, 21; and
    the Serpent, 21, 23
Ahaz, 90, 99, 101, 102; failure of to
    trust God, 91–92
Alexander, T. Desmond, 36n5,
    48nn7–8, 56n21, 143n2
Arnold, Bill T., 121

Asshur: and the building of impor-
    tant cities in northern Meso-
    potamia, 27, 27n3; and Hebrew
    'aššûr, 27n3
Assyria/Assyrians, 28; defeat of, 101;
    destruction of the northern king-
    dom of Israel in 722 BC by, 28, 93
Averbeck, Richard E., 52

Babel, 24–29; Abraham as a deliberate
    contrast with, 32; as the antithesis
    of the city of God, 25, 27, 29, 90;
    association of with aggressive
    human leadership or kingship,
    27–28; Babel/Babylon, 26–29;
    building of, 24–25; building of as
    typifying two different character-
    istics of humanity, 25; and God's
    fragmentation of humanity into
    different ethnic groups and na-
    tions, 29, 31; and Hebrew babel,
    26; and pride, 25–26; as the proto-
    typical godless city, 25, 28–29, 31;
    as the rival and opponent of the
    city of God, 27. See also Babylon,
    in the book of Revelation
Babylon, in the book of Revelation,
    153–55; as a cipher for Rome,
    154n14; as the "great prostitute,"
    154; symbolic meaning of, 154n14

Scripture Index

Short Studies in Biblical Theology Series

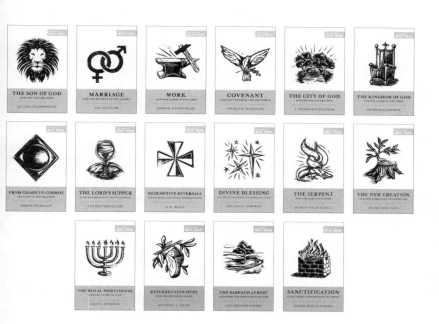

For more information, visit **crossway.org/ssbt**.